The Miracles of Jesus

David Otto

ABINGDON PRESS
Nashville

THE MIRACLES OF JESUS

by David Otto

ISBN 0-687-09020-2

00 01 02 03 04 05 06 07 08 09—10 9 8 7 6 5 4 3 2 1

MANUFACTURED IN THE UNITED STATES OF AMERICA

Contents

Meet the Writer

David Otto currently serves as associate professor of religion at Centenary College in Shreveport, Louisiana. Nationally recognized as a dynamic speaker and provocative scholar, David has published numerous works, including *Reality Check*, a guide for local churches in redesigning youth ministry for a new millennium. He can be seen regularly on the Odyssey Network in the long-running television series, *Scriptures Alive*, which explores social issues from biblical and theological perspectives.

A Word of Welcome

Welcome to THE MIRACLES OF JESUS, a study of the nature of miracles and of several of the miracle narratives in the Gospels and Acts. This study takes a fresh approach to investigating the miracles by using four keys to understanding:

- Miracles offer the participant and the observer a new historical perspective. Here we see the event in its own broad context.
- Miracles inevitably have consequences. What happens in the aftermath, and how does it affect the participant and the observer?
- Miracles evoke a social memory. One event reminds us of another and that prior happening helps us put an event into context and make meaning of the new.
- Miracles prompt us to talk about God and the insights we gain afresh each time we see or review how God has acted wondrously in our own lives or the lives of our forebears in the faith.

This study gives you ample opportunity to place yourself in God's unfolding story and to see not only what a miracle meant to the community of faith but also how that miracle supported and propelled that same community. These ancient miracles continue to inspire and direct our lives and our insight about God's grace in the world.

We invite you to delve deeply into this study of Jesus' miracles and pray that you will find a blessing in it.

How to Use This Resource

We hope you enjoy participating in this study, either on your own or with a group. We offer these hints and suggestions to make your study a success.

THE MIRACLES OF JESUS is a self-contained study with all the teaching/learning suggestions conveniently located on or near the main text to which they refer. They are identified with the same heading (or a close abbreviation) as the heading in the main text. In addition to your Bible, all you need to have a successful group or individual study session is provided for you in this book.

Some special features are provided as well, such as the **Bible 301** activities in the teaching helps. We usually think of the "101" designation as the beginning level; these "301" designations prompt you to dig deeper. In these instances you will be invited to look up Scriptures, key words, or concepts in a Bible dictionary, commentary, or atlas. On occasion, an added book or resource is cited that may be obtained from your local library or perhaps from your pastor. Those resources are extras; your study will be enriched by these added sources of information, but it is not dependent on them.

This study is intentionally invitational. In the closing activity, you are invited to do three things: to give prayerful consideration to your relationship to Jesus Christ and make or renew your commitment, to offer your own spoken prayers, and to pray with and for others. We trust you will participate in these activities as you feel comfortable and that you will use them as a challenge to grow more confident with prayer and with your covenant with Jesus Christ.

Session One

Four Keys to Understanding Miracles

Session Focus ■

Christians understand miracles in the modern world by using the miracles of Jesus as a template. Giving attention to the four keys or dimensions of the miracles of Jesus can assist believers and seekers in discovering the timeless wealth of these sacred stories.

Session Objective ■

To introduce four critical keys or dimensions of miracles within the Christian life: to offer historical perspective, to generate social aftermath, to function as social memory, and to teach us about the nature of God.

Session Preparation ■

After reading through the session for the first time, spend time looking through local newspapers, magazines, and periodicals for stories that might describe miracles. You may even think of special scenes from movies or novels that depict a wonderful, inexplicable event. Gather this material and use it to decorate your meeting room.

"There was a child who could not speak. He came to the temple [of Asklepios] for a voice. He sacrificed and performed the customary rituals. After this, the child, while he was bringing a torch to the God, was commanded, as he was looking at his father, to wait one year, and when he had gotten what he had wanted, to come back and offer the thank offering. The child suddenly said, 'I will wait.' And the father, astonished, ordered him to speak again. He spoke again. From this time he was healed" (The Epidauros Inscription, taken from a fourth-century B.C. temple of Asklepios. Cited in *Documents for the Study of the Gospels*, David R. Cartlidge and David L. Dungan, editors; Minneapolis: Fortress Press, 1994; page 152).

Throughout the ancient world, stories of miracles—and miracle workers—seemed quite popular. In the story cited above, the ancient physician Asklepios is remembered as a divine man who healed persons by the power of the gods, even after Asklepios had been dead for many decades. Asklepios was said to have raised the dead from their graves and the lame from their cots. It was also generally believed that Asklepios was born through a rather miraculous coupling: his mother was a mortal while his father was the famous god Apollo.

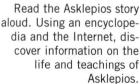
But these stories seem rather familiar to readers of the New Testament. Did Jesus have a miraculous birth? And what about all the healing stories in the four Gospels? Should the claims of divine power made on behalf of the followers of Asklepios in any way affect the proclamation of Christians concerning the work and power of Christ? How are we to understand the miracle stories of Jesus found in the Bible?

What is a miracle? Are miracles still occurring in our lives today? To what extent should the person who believes in Christ Jesus expect miracles? And what are the characteristics of a Christ-centered miracle?

So many questions. It is my hope that we can explore some of these issues in this book. Within this initial session, we will investigate the notion of miracles and what possible problems arise when we propose to define such an event.

What Is a Miracle?

On the surface, answering this question seems a simple task: miracles are those wonderful acts of God. Many Christian theologians throughout history would agree with this statement. In fact, in the Holy Bible the Hebrew and Greek words we generally translate as *miracle* would be best rendered as "signs and wonders" suggesting God's presence in the world.

But this definition has some significant problems. First, miracles seem to be selective in nature, occurring at specific times to specific people at specific places. If miracles suggest the presence of God in the world, why don't miracles occur with greater regularity? Should the lack of miracles in the world suggest the absence of God?

Second, modern science has aptly

does not have God at the center of it be a real miracle? Explain.

Biographies of famous persons like Julius Caesar and Plato, written well before the birth of Jesus, declare them "born of a virgin." How should the Christian understand such claims?

What Is a Miracle? ■

How would you define a miracle? Write these ideas on a sheet of poster paper or on a chalkboard.

Using the "Gallery," look for the best representation of your understanding of a miracle.

Why, do you think, do miracles not occur with greater regularity? If we do not see miracles, does that suggest that God is absent or no longer desires to interact with us? Explain.

How might the Holy Spirit work through medical technology to produce miracles?

Can a wonderful miracle for one be another person's source of misery? Why or why not?

How should the Christian understand the miracles that occur in the lives of persons who practice other religions?

explained many events that our ancestors considered miracles. Illness is now viewed by most Westerners as a sign of infection rather than sin, for instance, with healing seen as the work of modern medical technology more often than the work of the Holy Spirit. Is *miracle* just a term we use to describe events that modern science has yet to explain?

Third, what is considered "wonderful" by one group of persons may be experienced as "horrible" by another. The miracle of rain for farmers, for instance, can also bring flooding and death for others. Can one person's miracle be another person's source of misery?

Finally, what about other groups who have historically declared the work of miracles? Should the healing stories attributed to the ancient physician Asklepios, for example, be rejected as "miraculous" since they do not lay claim to the presence of God? What of the miracle stories concerning the actions of the Buddha or any other religious figure?

I want to suggest four insights or keys concerning miracles. These observations will be used as a template or method by which we will explore the miracles performed by Jesus. Hopefully, these keys will offer guidelines to our discussion, helping us navigate among the thorny issues raised above.

Key One: Miracles as Historical Perception

Last year a member of my local church was diagnosed with breast cancer. Nancy and her family were initially devastated by the news. Over the next seven months, Nancy underwent extensive chemotherapy, radiation treatments, and two surgeries. During the second surgery, however, it was discovered that the

Ask one person to read aloud Nancy's story while others close their eyes and listen closely.

Explain the adage, "Perspective is everything." How might it apply to our understanding of miracles in the world? If the perception of a miracle should lead to praise of God, what should be your response to the "Gallery" miracles? How might your small group give praise to God for Nancy's miracle?

Spend a few moments designing an appropriate response, then engage it. Ideas include prayer, a brief worship service, and rededicating one's life to Jesus Christ.

cancer had spread. At this point most of Nancy's doctors surrendered hope and suggested she enroll in a terminal care program.

But family and church members refused to give up so easily. Even while Nancy experienced a deep sense of hopelessness, the community of faith prayed to God on her behalf, visited Nancy daily, and offered her Communion on a weekly basis.

Then something wonderful occurred: Nancy's cancer went into remission. For the last few months, the health of this forty-three-year-old woman with three children has improved. In fact, Nancy has even been seen swimming, playing a round of golf, and attending church. From the perspective of members of our church family, Nancy experienced the miraculous presence of God.

The story of Nancy reminds me of numerous healing narratives associated with Jesus. With a simple touch, Jesus cured the blind and lame (Matthew 21:14; Mark 8:22-26) and brought miracles to the multitudes (Matthew 14:34-36; Luke 6:17-19). But these declarations of miracles rarely attempt to describe *how* the healing occurred. While the presence of Jesus appears crucial for the emergence of a miracle, the actual dynamics are rarely explored within the Gospels. We are left to draw the conclusion that the *perception* (the "what") of miracles seemed more important to the New Testament writers than did the *process* (the "how").

Likewise, as a member of Nancy's faith community, I do not find myself wondering how a form of inoperable cancer suddenly went into remission. Instead, I find myself giving testimony to the fact that it did and giving God the credit for the healing.

The miracle narratives of the New Testament celebrate the perceptions of early

Christians who saw incredible events performed in the name of Jesus Christ. Such testimony gave support to the truths being promoted by these small communities. While the presence of the living Christ was a prerequisite for the occurrence of miracles, the focus of these historic proclamations is usually placed on the fact that miracles happen. The questions of motivation (the "Why" questions) or mechanics ("How" miracles occur in the world) rarely appear as the central purpose of a miracle story.

No Explanation Necessary

Many Christian theologians, scholars, and believers have found themselves preoccupied with the "Why" and "How" questions, however. Some persons have opted for such explanations as, "Well, if that person had just had a bit more faith, then he would have received a miracle" or "Miracles are natural events in the world yet to be explained by science." Such wondering—while holding interest for the modern thinker—appears to have little relevance to the biblical stories of Jesus' miracles. Instead, these sacred events proclaim the presence of the living Christ (the "What"), begging the reader to ask two deeper questions:

- So what happens next? What is the "aftermath" of a miracle?
- What should these miracle stories help me remember or recall?

Key Two:
Miracles as Aftermath

Recall Nancy, the wonderful friend I mentioned above. The miraculous healing of Nancy not only changed her life but also challenged the lives of those persons around

No Explanation Necessary ■

Read Matthew 21:14, Mark 8:22-26, Matthew 14:34-36, and Luke 6:17-19. What do these passages have in common? Does their lack of detail suggest that these reports are any less authentic than others?

Are the "why" and "how" of a miracle important to you? If you could answer those questions, would the miracle still be miraculous? Explain.

Key Two: ■
Aftermath

Ask a group member to read aloud the next segment of Nancy's story. Invite the participants to list the specific changes brought about by the miracle. Note the changes in the lives of family and church members.

Have you ever been in a similar situation? What was that like? What happened? How did you deal with it? In what ways was life changed for you and/or for others?

her. The members of Nancy's family had to adjust to her change in health and wellness. No longer an invalid, Nancy could—and demanded to—do things for herself. Her husband, Ralph, was being asked to resume marital responsibilities he had dismissed as inappropriate several months prior. The three children were remembering what "having a mommy" was like before the illness, but did not wish to surrender the sense of independence Nancy's illness had offered them. And her church family struggled with shifting gears, treating Nancy like a "regular" person rather than a "sick" one.

Sadly, most of our members have had a difficult time with this shift, so much so that Nancy has stopped attending Sunday service. Over coffee last week, Nancy confessed, "I just can't stand how they seem so incapable of treating me like a functional human being. Most folks just keep asking me the same question over and over: 'How are we feeling today, Nancy?' using that patronizing tone of voice. It is as if my presence just makes us both uncomfortable."

Meeting the Consequences

How would you describe the aftermath of Nancy's story so far? What emotional impact does it seem to carry to this point?

When have you found yourself dealing with the "aftermath" of a situation, such as the one you mentioned earlier?

Meeting the Consequences

All miracles bring about *an aftermath*, a secondary set of events that often leads to major changes in relationships and the physical world. Such experiences of an aftermath contain both good and bad experiences, no matter how "wonderful" the miracle seems to be. For the story of Nancy, the aftermath involved everything from removing railings from the bathroom wall to losing some dear friends who could not deal with the new situation. Husband, children, friends, and colleagues changed in the midst of Nancy's transformation.

The stories of an aftermath can be devas-

What tools or techniques do you use in managing change or ambiguity? How can a miracle for one person or group be experienced as disruption or discord by another?

Suppose the televised healing was not authentic, but staged to provoke a particular response. What happens when a miracle doesn't seem to "stick," when it is short-lived or is an outright hoax? How, do you think, do witnesses to this miracle deal with dashed expectations and hopes?

What would such chicanery do to support or deny the possibility of a "real miracle"?

tating, introducing ambiguity and change into what was perhaps a terrible—but stable—situation. Maybe the fear of ambiguity keeps us from exploring this deeper dimension of miracles: how miracles introduce radical change to the world.

A few weeks ago I found myself surfing the television channels late at night. As I flipped channels, using the remote control, I came upon a broadcast of some type of Christian worship experience. I stopped clicking and watched for several minutes. The pastor/leader motioned for a member of the congregation to step forward; the individual came to the pastor, assisted by a set of crutches and two persons. After praying over the physically impaired individual, the pastor slapped the forehead of the "sinner," shouting, "Be healed in the name of Christ Jesus." The crutches fell aside as the person fell to the floor—only to stand up moments later, dancing and crying with joy. A miracle had occurred; the lame person could walk again.

While I do not wish to doubt the sincerity of either the pastor or the other participants in the broadcast, I did find myself thinking about the question of aftermath. What happened to those lives over the next few weeks or months? Television and movies rarely show us such stories of aftermath, apparently not good for the ratings. Fortunately, most of the biblical narratives concerning miracles have "built-in" aftermath stories, clues the ancient writers leave for the observant readers who want to know "what happened next."

The Ten Lepers ▪

Read Luke 17:11-19. What are the ironies in this story? How does the miracle reflect on Jesus' power

The Ten Lepers

Read Luke 17:11-19, a great healing story. But look closer. The healing of the ten men (nine Galilean Jews and one Samaritan) seems secondary to the "rest of the story"; only the

and ability? What does it teach us about human life?

Spend a few moments thinking about the life of the Samaritan. How do you think the Samaritan acted two weeks after the healing event? two years after?

How can current shifts in health care practices be compared to Jesus' disruption of the medical practices of his day? How should the Christian determine the value of such changes in modern health care?

Samaritan returned to Jesus to give him thanks and praise. What happened to the other nine men? Why did they fail to return to give praise to the Jewish Messiah? Further, the men were healed outside of the typical association with a Jewish priest. The aftermath: Jesus' healing of the nine Galilean Jews disrupted the standard system by which illnesses were diagnosed and healing occurred.

In short, Jesus' actions suggest the institution of the healing priests to be obsolete, if not totally bankrupt. In this story, it is the aftermath that makes the miracle significant: Non-Jews can become part of God's family through Jesus Christ, and the old Jewish system of health and wellness is usurped.

Most stories of aftermath deal with shifts in personal, social, cultural, and spiritual relationships. Indeed, many modern biblical scholars point out that the miracle stories in the Gospels are unique from other miracle stories due to the existence of the aftermath dimension. By exploring the aftermath of the miracles of Jesus, we will see just how many lives have been changed through his actions.

Key Three: Social Memory ■

Read the next section of the Nancy story in silence. List key words from Bible stories, movies, classic literature, or other sources that come to mind while reading. Discuss these key words and the stories behind them.

Key Three: Miracles Function as Social Memory

I remember when I first heard of the miraculous remission of Nancy's cancer; I was teaching an adult Sunday school class. One of the members had just spoken with Ralph, who had decided to stay home with Nancy and the children. During the rather rushed conversation, Ralph related the welcomed news that the doctors had discovered the cancer was in remission. "In fact," claimed the class member who had spoken to Ralph, "the doctors say the cancer has faded away almost completely. Ralph was crying with joy."

While joining in Ralph's celebration of the

How do miracle stories function as social memory for you? In your experience, are these events or stories bonding experiences in some way? How do they affect your faith?

good news, many class members began to rehearse their remembrance of "older" good news: stories of previous healings; anecdotes about famous miracles from world history; and the best "Old Good News" of all, the healing stories involving Jesus. Somehow all of these stories, including the story of Nancy, were connected in the minds and hearts of the class members.

The most recent miracle in a sense assisted us in recalling all the other times that such wonderful signs had occurred in the name of Christ Jesus. The miracle story became a recent link in an endless, historical chain of miracle events that gave testimony to the presence of Christ in the world. Through Nancy, we remembered the basic proclamation of Christian faith: Christ has always been with us.

How do you rehearse the stories of the Christian faith? Name three ways in which you might share the story of Christ during the next week.

But I also noticed something else: the way in which we told our own remembrances of miracles reflected the form or style in which we were taught to tell such stories. Many persons who were familiar with the Gospel accounts, for instance, told stories about the work of healers, usually incorporating some dialogue that had taken place between the one who was sick and the one who came to heal. Those persons who seemed less familiar with the biblical text told miracle stories reflected in recent movies they had seen or books they had read. The stories were more detailed, had subplots, even romantic conclusions.

Sacred Stories ■

Read 2 Kings 4:42-44 and Mark 6:30-44. What happens? How does the story of Elisha compare to the feeding miracle in Mark? Why would Jesus replicate an ancient miracle? What

Sacred Stories

Many of these students would start their story with the line, "Do you remember that movie? You remember the scene where. . . ." Heads would nod in affirmation and we would lean forward in our chairs, waiting for the storyteller to reenact the film's critical moments for us.

makes a miracle "Christian"?

How might familiarity with the older story affect belief in the current story? How do these older stories trigger responses or memories that enhance our faith?

There were other reported miracle workers in Jesus' day (and before and after, as well). Many of them were charlatans. How does the miracle claim authenticity?

The class was tapping into a deep set of memories that came from a variety of sources. And Nancy's miracle served as the impetus for our sacred moment of rehearsing. Many modern biblical scholars believe that the miracle stories of Jesus were written with this process in mind. The writers intentionally fashioned their stories to "trigger" a set of memories within the ancient listener or reader.

Often, the miracle stories of Jesus reminded the reader of specific stories from the Old Testament. For instance, read Mark 6:30-44. This miracle narrative appears in some form within all four Gospel texts. Now read 2 Kings 4:42-44. An early story about multiplying loaves! Early Christians who took the study of Hebrew Scripture seriously would recognize these two stories as strangely similar. Why would Jesus' miracles be so reminiscent of the actions of the old prophet Elisha?

On other occasions, however, the stories seem highly reminiscent of miracle stories that would have been popular with the original audiences of the ancient world: stories of miraculous healers, workers of wonders, and persons who claimed special relationships with the gods. The story of Asklepios at the beginning of this session serves as a great example. Jesus is like this ancient healer; their actions are similar. But Jesus is greater than Asklepios, for the divine nature of Jesus is bigger, stronger, and more authentic than that of Asklepios. By guiding the process of memory, the writers of the New Testament offer a critical commentary on the miracles that precede the work of Jesus and how Christians should understand the miracles that follow.

Key Four:
Talk About God ■

If given the opportunity, what questions would you like to ask God concerning miracles? Write these questions on a large sheet of poster paper and display the list throughout the remaining sessions. As each session begins to address these questions, place some type of mark or symbol by the question.

Must God violate the physical laws of the universe to perform a miracle? Explain.

Is there any such thing as someone who "deserves" a miracle? Who could possibly "deserve" one? Explain. Is worthiness ever a consideration in God's interaction with humankind? Explain.

Must miracles always suggest a divine purpose for the recipient or for a witness?

Key Four:
Miracles Talk About God

As our adult Sunday school class shared our stories regarding miracles, a significant set of questions emerged: Who is God? What is God's purpose for our lives? How does God intervene in the lives of common people? The topic of miracles inevitably led to a discussion of the nature of God. Did the topic emerge by accident? I decided to conduct a bit of research.

Christian theologians and philosophers throughout the ages found their descriptions and discourse concerning miracles always led to a more basic set of questions concerning the nature and identity of God. Must God violate the physical laws of the universe to perform a miracle? If miracles are special moments of intervention by God, does this mean God is usually absent from the world? What kind of God would favor some persons with a miracle and not others, especially when many of the unfavored people seem so deserving? Must miracles always suggest a divine purpose for the recipient, or could they simply function as random "gifts" built into the fabric of creation, occurring without concern for the specific individual or individuals involved, for the purpose of generating veneration and worship among a larger group of human subjects? Do, perhaps, miracles say more about the miracle worker than about the one to whom the miracle occurs?

Getting Into ■
"God Talk"

In what way might the study of miracles be a primer of sorts to help you engage in "God talk"?

Getting Into "God Talk"

Such history of "God talk," or theology, supports a unique hypothesis: that miracle narratives of Jesus function as a primary avenue by which Christian communities begin the conversation of theology. While most persons in that adult Sunday school

Bible 301 ☐

Read Matthew 21:18-22, the story of the cursed fig tree. Have on hand a Bible commentary to help explain this event. Why does Jesus cause the tree to die? If the fig tree serves as a symbol for something in your life, what would it be?

What responsibility might come with the power to destroy life? Spend time exploring this question: How has freedom and technology provided humans with the ability to destroy individual lives and entire cities?

Should the ability to destroy necessitate the use of that ability? How might restraint be viewed as a miracle?

class I taught would resist calling themselves "theologians," all of them expressed key ideas and questions concerning the nature and purpose of God in our lives. Maybe the study of the miracles of Jesus serves as a primer of sorts, an introduction to the fundamental questions of Christian theology. In this way, Christians throughout the ages have engaged in the deeper "study" of God.

For example, let's look at a rather cryptic miracle: the cursing of the fig tree (Matthew 21:18-22). On the surface, the actions of Jesus hardly seem "miraculous"; the tree withers and dies. A destructive act, to say the least. Poor tree. And who does not like figs? What a sweet treat, for ancient and modern folk alike.

Jesus then tells the disciples, "Truly I tell you, if you have faith and do not doubt, not only will you do what has been done to the fig tree [curse and destroy], but even if you say to this mountain [the entire city of Jerusalem], "Be lifted up and thrown into the sea," it will be done" (21:21). What kind of doubtless faith would lead to the acquisition of such a destructive force? What kind of savior—or followers—would slay an innocent tree or the famous city of Jerusalem, with all of its inhabitants? This parable raises many subtle but substantive questions concerning the darker nature of God and the ministry Jesus intends for his disciples. By reading the miracle narratives closely, we can enter a historical conversation that links us to the earliest listeners and readers of these Gospels, a discussion of the mystery of God.

Using the Keys ■

In the sessions that follow, we will use these four keys to unlock the deeper, somewhat hidden dimensions of the miracles of

analyze one or more of the items found in your "Gallery" or one of the miracles mentioned in this session. What insights and questions did the use of the four keys generate?

Jesus. And you will be asked to use these same keys to analyze the "miracle moments" in your life. Maybe Christ is working in your life this very moment. Through the use of our four insights or keys, maybe you can open yourself to what God is saying to you.

Closing Prayer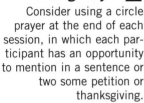

Consider using a circle prayer at the end of each session, in which each participant has an opportunity to mention in a sentence or two some petition or thanksgiving.

The miracles show us dramatically that God can and does work in startling and intimate ways with humankind. Take some time in prayer to consider your own relationship with God and then make or renew your commitment.

Close with your circle prayer, followed by this group prayer: "Precious God who brings about many signs and wonders, open our hearts and minds to your presence. When we open ourselves to the grace of your Son, Jesus Christ, great things happen. Amen."

For Next Week

Ask group members to bring baby pictures with them for Session Two (see "Session Preparation," page 20).

Session Two

Miraculous Births, Miraculous Lives

Session Focus ■

The birth narratives of Jesus call us to affirm our kinship with both God and one another. Through the birth, life, death, and resurrection of Jesus, Christians become blood relatives with one another. Learning to treat one another as "kinfolk" emerges as the imperative task.

Session Objective ■

To use the four keys introduced in Session One to explore the genealogies and birth stories of Jesus found in the Gospels of Matthew and Luke.

Session Preparation ■

Ask persons to come to this session with a collection of baby pictures to share. These photos may be of their own children, nieces and nephews, grandchildren, other relatives, or themselves.

Decorate a tabletop using these photographs, along with two candles and a Bible. You may also wish to decorate the room with your favorite Christmas items, such as family orna-

Wonderful signs and events foretold and shadowed the birth of Jesus, as told by the Gospel writers. Throughout the ages, Christians have celebrated, remembered, and reflected on this incredible set of miracles. Within this session, we will explore the birth of Jesus as a significant set of miracles designed to encourage both believers and seekers to understand the nature and destiny of this peasant of Galilee who was the Christ. To assist us in our investigation, we will use the four keys described in Session One:

• Miracles as Historical Perception
• Miracles as Aftermath
• Miracles Function as Social Memory
• Miracles Talk About God

Matthew's Account:
A Messiah Born to Reenact and Fulfill

The Gospel of Matthew opens with a genealogy that traces the birth of Jesus through the house of King David to the birth of Abraham, the father of the Jewish faith. Read Matthew 1:1-17. Most scholars notice several items concerning this family tree. First, the family tree leaves out several generations; mixing and matching family lines and births in ways that appear contrary to the Old Testament. Odd? Definitely. Why? Keep reading.

ments, a Nativity scene, or Christmas carols playing in the background. Who cares if it's the middle of summer? We will be celebrating the wonderful birth of Jesus.

For the "Bible 301" activities, you will need a Bible dictionary and a commentary on the Book of Luke.

Choose from among these activities and discussion starters to plan your lesson.

Matthew's Account ■

Briefly swap birth stories and share photographs and genealogies. Keep this activity short, but festive and joyful.

Pray together, asking for God's guidance as you explore the incredible birth of Jesus. Ask God to help you maintain the sense of celebration and joy felt during the opening exercise.

Describe the most recent birth that has touched your life. If you have a genealogy of your family, share it with other participants. Take a look at a genealogy, either of a participant or the one cited in Matthew 1:1-17. Typically, what purpose would a family tree serve? Why might persons find it meaningful to know the names, locations, and actions of their ancestors? Why might it be important to pay attention

The second thing we notice is the structure and sequence of the tree members. The genealogy divides into three separate units, each of fourteen generations. Unit One takes us from Abraham to the birth of David, who would be the legendary king of Israel. The second unit moves us along in time until the fall of Judah in 587 B.C. The final unit picks up with the Babylonian Exile, culminating with the birth of Jesus. Why the three units of fourteen generations? Could it be an important clue?

Finally, this genealogy refers to four women: Tamar (Genesis 38), Rahab (Joshua 2), Ruth (Ruth 1–4), and Bathsheba, "the wife of Uriah" (2 Samuel 11–12). Tamar, the daughter-in-law of Judah, pretended to be a temple prostitute to force Judah to keep his promises. Rahab was another prostitute whose unusual actions and wit helped Joshua conquer the land of Canaan. Ruth was a widowed Moabite who found favor with Boaz and the followers of God. Bathsheba was the wife of another man when David lusted after her and engineered Uriah's death in order to have Bathsheba as his own. Why would Matthew mention these rather unconventional women?

The genealogy of Matthew offers us a wonderful synopsis of the purpose for the birth narrative that follows. By constructing a family tree that bears a few obvious holes, Matthew is telling the reader, "Pay attention to the details; look closely."

An Illustrious History

On closer investigation, we notice that this family tree of Jesus records the names of some of the most famous movers and shakers throughout Jewish history. This genealogy reads like a "Who's Who" in ancient Israel.

to these details? How many previous generations do you know by name in your family history?

An Illustrious History ■

Form four groups and assign the Old Testament story of one of the four biblical women to each group: Tamar (Genesis 38), Rahab (Joshua 2), Bathsheba (2 Samuel 11–12), or Ruth (Ruth 1–4). Read these selections aloud to the whole group. On poster paper, record the memorable actions of each of the characters.

Bible 301 ☐

Use a Bible dictionary to find other references to these four women to get a more complete picture of their lives and involvement in Hebrew history. Add that information to your record.

Name two women, members of your "family tree," whom you remember as critical characters to the shape and destiny of your family. How did God work through these women?

Using a Bible dictionary, looking up the names in Matthew's genealogy. For what specific reasons do we remember these persons?

As a result, it raises an important question in our minds: To what degree will this baby grow up to be like Abraham, Isaac, or the other famous leaders of the faith? Should we expect Matthew's Jesus to demonstrate all the wonderful virtues of these earlier sacred leaders?

Our second insight concerning the structure and sequence of these names confirms this first observation. The three units or sections of the genealogy could correspond to the three sections of the Hebrew Bible: the Law, the Prophets, and the Writings. In fact, the genealogy cites famous persons mentioned in all three sections of the Hebrew Bible. Further, Matthew quotes the Hebrew Bible (he apparently has a Greek translation of the Hebrew text) more than any of the other Gospel writers. Most scholars believe that Matthew intends both ancient and modern readers to take note of this heavy use of citation and the borrowed structure of the Hebrew Bible to make a single but important point: Jesus will be born to fulfill all Jewish expectation; to deliver on all promises God had made throughout the centuries to the Jewish people and recorded in the sacred Hebrew text. Hence, throughout Matthew you notice variations on the line, "He did this to fulfill Scripture." The miracle of the birth rests in Jesus' ability to make good on all of God's promises to the people of God.

But why the four women? What an oddity within the genealogy. And why these women, all of whom found themselves in unconventional, unusual relationships and occupations? In short, it seems Matthew may wish to identify a particular promise made by God: to include women as full and complete members of the family of God.

In the ancient world, women were consid-

How important is the Old Testament (and our Old Testament forebears) to your faith? How might Matthew answer the same question?

How has the role and status of women changed over the last fifty years? How might female identity be shaped and altered by current social and world events?

Matthew's Birth Narrative ■

Read Matthew 1:20-21. Why might God resist consulting Mary about this birth? Name some of the feelings Mary might have experienced. Why might Matthew fail to mention, as Luke did, that God sent an angel to speak to Mary about what was to come?

Try to imagine (even if you are a man) what it would be like to be a woman of Mary's world, and assume for a moment that Matthew's account of the birth of Jesus is the only one. As a person with little power or prerogative, what might it mean to you that the husband who has been secured for you has been informed about your miraculous, and evidently uninvited, pregnancy? How would you feel?

ered property of their fathers then of the men to whom they were sold (husbands). By including the names of these independent women within the genealogy, Matthew declares that the ministry and life of Jesus will bring about radical changes for the women who have found themselves oppressed by others and disconnected from the faith. Like Tamar, Rahab, Ruth, and Bathsheba women will play a significant, unconventional role in the creation of God's kingdom.

Matthew's Birth Narrative

Given the last statement made about women, it seems odd that the birth narrative told by Matthew fails to include the voice of Mary, that the angel of the Lord only appears to Joseph and then only in a dream (see Matthew 1:20-21). Matthew fails to record any conversation God may have had with Mary. Further, while the angel of the Lord reveals to Joseph that Mary is with child "conceived by the Holy Spirit," we have no idea how Mary feels about this divine pregnancy. We have to rely on Luke for this voice and perspective.

But there seems great value in looking at the Matthew account separately. In this version, Mary is very much like most women of the ancient world: owned by a father and promised (betrothed) to a man she most probably did not know. Marriages were arranged contracts in the ancient world, designed by fathers as business contracts that brought unity between two family lines for the sake of economic and social gain. In this sense, Jesus is born to the typical woman.

Key One ■

Read Matthew 5:17-19. Try to place the birth of Jesus in its historical context. What were the hopes and expectations? How does Matthew begin to tell us how these expectations are being met, even if in ways that had not been anticipated?

Key One

Using the four keys from Session One, we can begin to unpack the riches of this miracle narrative. Our first key involves reading a miracle story as a *historical proclamation* of the truth of Jesus Christ. Indeed, when the birth narrative of Matthew is linked to the genealogy that begins the Gospel, we hear the wonderful proclamation of the nature of Jesus: a man born to fulfill all Jewish expectation and promises. And as we read beyond this birth story into the heart of the Gospel, we find ample evidence to support our assumption. Read Matthew 5:17-19, for instance. Unlike in the other Gospels, Jesus declares that "not one letter of the law" (Torah, the first section of the Hebrew Bible) will go unfulfilled.

Key Two ■

Think about the last pageant, drama, movie, or play you saw in which the character Mary was depicted. List five words that describe her appearance, behavior, and temperament. Now select five additional words that describe the Mary found in the Gospel of Matthew. How do your lists compare? How might you account for similarities and differences? What evidence of "aftermath" do you see?

Key Two

Using the second key, miracles invite *aftermath*, our attention swings back to Mary. While introduced as an ordinary women, her life takes a rather unorthodox and unique set of twists and turns. She finds herself pregnant through a miraculous union with God by the Holy Spirit. She gives birth to Jesus, who comes to save the people from sin and despair. And, as we follow Mary throughout the Gospel of Matthew, she begins to exert a radical sense of independence, acting in an atypical fashion to women of her day, but more like the women from the genealogy!

While the character of Joseph fades into the background, Mary emerges as an independent presence. Imagine what the other women (and men) would have thought of Mary: "Wasn't she the quiet, submissive woman owned by Joseph? Now look at her! Why, she is acting like a man: independent, self-assured, public, unashamed." Just like Tamar, Rahab, Ruth, and Bathsheba!

Key Three

Review the information about other miraculous births that Matthew's audience would likely have known, as well as what you recall about Greek and Roman mythology. What similarities do you see?

How is the birth of Jesus different from, say, the birth of Hercules, who had a human mother and the god Zeus as his father? How would the Israelites' acquaintance with this mythology predispose them (or not) to want or expect a half man/half god messiah?

The birth narrative would evoke a social memory of these other births that were attributed to miracle. What effect is there on this social memory when what is evoked is perceived as something false? (For example, Hercules' miraculous birth might come to mind in the context of the birth story of another god's son, but we regard Hercules as fiction.) How would Matthew's readers know Jesus was the real son of the real God if Hercules, for example, was not?

Key Three

Miracles can also offer themselves as *devices of social memory*. What events in history or ancient literature should this miraculous birth bring to mind? And for what purpose? Strangely, the Old Testament offers little resource at this point. Jewish communities throughout the centuries who awaited a messiah generally would not have expected somebody born through the pairing of a human woman with a god.

While the genealogy recalls the entirety of the Hebrew Bible and, with it, Jewish expectations for the coming of a messiah, the birth narrative itself would have struck a strictly Jewish audience as peculiar. What would have been recalled would be the numerous stories of miraculous and virgin births attributed to Roman emperors and chronicled throughout the myths of the Greco-Roman world. Stories of Octavian Augustus, Julius Caesar, Hercules, Athena, and even Alexander the Great. Why would the God of Abraham, Isaac, Jacob, and David behave like one of the Greek or Roman gods, impregnating a human woman for the sake of giving birth to a son who would be half-human/half-divine?

Matthew knew the birth of Jesus would remind his worldly, educated listeners and readers of these other so-called miracle births; that was exactly the point. Most of the people attributed such births were considered to possess great powers of leadership, wisdom, and healing. It was also thought, upon death, that these saviors would ascend to the heavens (or Mount Olympus) to spend eternity with the god who was their father. If the readers continued to explore Matthew's sacred biography of Jesus, they would discover that Jesus fulfills all the requirements for a

Greco-Roman savior, but with a critical difference: Jesus not only outperformed them all, he was the real son of a real God. Jesus had come not just to fulfill Jewish history and expectation but to make good on promises of salvation made to all humankind (even by false gods), demonstrating once and for all the supremacy of God and God's love for the entire world.

Key Four ■
What does this miraculous birth tell you about the nature of God? Why would God have impregnated Mary in a way that overtly resembled the actions of other gods? (Note that unlike the Olympian gods, for example, there is nothing specifically sexual in God's act; in Creation, God spoke and willed something to happen, and it did.)

Has there ever been a time in your life when you felt that God "wore a mask," showing only one aspect of God's nature? Describe that moment. How do you understand the triune nature of God?

Read Genesis 32. When was the last time you struggled with God? When have you "worn a mask" in the presence of God? Why did you do it? What was the result?

Key Four

Finally, the miraculous birth of Jesus, as recorded by Matthew, raises important questions about the *nature of God*. Why did God impregnate Mary in a way that resembled the actions of other gods? How are we to understand the relationship between God and Jesus as distinct but one? What is the "Holy Spirit," and what is the Spirit's relationship to God/Jesus? These questions suggest ideas regarding the Trinity: Father, Son and Holy Spirit.

For hundreds of years the Christian church has debated on how these three personas can reflect a singular God. One solution, borrowed from ancient theater, involved imaging the Father, Son, and Holy Spirit as "Three Faces of God": three unique masks that the Holy One wore while communing with God's loved ones. But questions continue: Why the need for such masks or personas? What kind of God cannot be experienced "in the raw," like Jacob did when he wrestled God on the banks of the river Jabbok (Genesis 32)? Had God somehow changed between the time of Jacob and the time of Mary? And why come into the world at that particular time, in that particular place? What was so special about the early part of the first century and Palestine?

Luke: Miracle Birth ▐

What does it mean to celebrate the birth of Jesus as a miracle? Knowing that the word *miracle* in the original New Testament Greek literally conveys the notion of a sign with explosive possibilities, how does the birth of Jesus serve as an "explosion" in your life?

How would the difference in audience affect the way the Gospel writers told their stories?

Review the information in "No Birth, No Problem." What effect would the notion of Jewish adoptionism have on the need for a birth narrative?

Imagine that God would allow a new Gospel story to be written and told to twenty-first–century persons who had never known of the birth of Jesus. In groups of two or three, choose the context (the world is a big and diverse place). Then rewrite the Gospel in a way that would make it relevant and compelling for someone who had never heard it. (You can't change the information; just the way it is told and the details that are included.) Compare stories. What new insights come to light?

Luke: Miracle Birth for a Different Audience

Most modern biblical scholars assume that Luke borrows from both the Gospels of Mark and Matthew to fashion his sacred biography of Jesus. While Mark does not record a birth narrative (see "No Birth, No Problem," below, for possible reasons why), Luke does seem aware of Matthew's record of the special, divine event.

Matthew and Luke wrote to two different audiences: Matthew to a group of followers of Jesus who were Jewish; Luke to a predominantly non-Jewish (or *Gentile*) group. Luke's special problem was that Gentiles did not believe in the concept of a Jewish Messiah; they were not Jewish. So Luke's biography would need to express the truth of the living Christ a bit differently. As a result, Luke's birth account became a poetic, universalized story about the coming of the Savior for the entire world. While retaining a few of the critical aspects from Matthew, Luke focuses on the universalizing aspect of the miracle: this birth is a miracle for the entire world.

"No Birth, No Problem"

While Luke and Matthew include a birth narrative, the Gospel of Mark omits such a story. Instead, Mark begins his biography of Jesus with the miracle of the baptism. So, why not discuss the birth of Jesus? Most modern scholars assume that Mark's original audience was first-century Jews. These keen readers would be expecting a Jewish Messiah, a man anointed by oil for the particular tasks of deliverance and salvation. Within Jewish circles, messiahs were born like everybody else. Perhaps they would need to trace their family history to the house of David. But a messiah was a messiah because of what he did after being anointed a messiah. This group of ancient persons, known as Jewish Adoptionists, assumed that Jesus was "adopted" as God's beloved son at baptism rather than at birth. If Mark wrote for such an original audience, he would not be required to discuss the birth and boyhood years of Jesus.

Luke's Genealogy

Luke's Genealogy ■

Review Matthew 1:1-17 and Luke 3:23-38. Compare and contrast these genealogies of Jesus, and list their specific differences. Why do you think these differences exist? How do these two stories reflect the audience to whom they were originally addressed?

What would it mean for you to call Jesus your "brother" (key one: historical perception)? How might such an appellation or title affect the way you treat other family members or relatives?

What does it mean to say that all humans have the blood of Adam racing through their veins (key two: aftermath)? How might such a proclamation affect the way we treat all persons in the world?

Notice the vast differences in Luke's genealogy (3:23-38) and Matthew's (1:1-17). Technically speaking, it seems impossible to reconcile these two family trees. Luke creates a genealogy for the same reason as Matthew: to declare the reason for the miracle of Jesus' birth. A quick analysis suggests possible connections between Luke's family tree of Jesus and what occurs within the Gospel.

First, Luke traces the birth of Jesus to the first human being, Adam. If we follow the reasoning of Matthew at this point, we could assume that Luke—like Matthew—wanted to tell the reader something about the destiny of Jesus: that Jesus will be the fulfillment of all of humankind, a universal savior rather than just the Jewish Messiah who makes a secondary appeal to the Gentiles (non-Jews).

A second observation concerning the genealogy: Luke adds new names to the listing: Heli, Matthat, Melchi, Jannai, and others. These names do not appear anywhere in the Old Testament. And these names seem strangely *foreign*, at least to the ears of a Palestinian Jewish community; most are not of Hebrew origin.

While Matthew's family history of Jesus focuses on persons of Jewish descent, Luke generated a multiethnic, multicultural listing.

On a large sheet of poster paper, list the responsibilities of kinship: What should those persons related by blood do for one another (key three: social memory)? According to Luke's genealogy, to whom are we related? What does that mean to you?

This Jesus—for Luke—must be a Savior for the entire world, embracing all nationalities, races, ethnicities, and cultures. Jesus has the entire human family as his ancestors.

Using our four keys, the genealogy of Luke offers the careful reader a wonderful series of prophetic declarations. First (historical perception), Luke proclaims the historical *Jesus as offspring of the world while being Savior for the world.* No longer a simple Galilean peasant who came to save the Jews oppressed by Rome, Jesus—within the Gospel of Luke—will focus his attention on the world at large, many of whom would have been distant relatives, regardless of nationality.

The second key, miracle as aftermath, becomes obvious: If Luke's genealogy should be embraced as accurate, we all are *related by blood* to Jesus. How can this be? Simple. Luke's family tree focuses on "branches" that diverge from the historical "trunk" of Adam, the first human. These family lines branch off throughout the centuries, taking the Jesus lineage with it. The same blood that gives life and authority to Jesus continues to bring life and authority to all human beings. Regardless of race, gender, belief, nationality, ability, or heritage, *all* persons—through Luke's genealogy—can claim Jesus as kin because all of us come from Adam, the primordial ancestor. (This could make gift buying for the holidays difficult, however!)

Spend a moment thinking about the last time you participated in Holy Communion: the body and blood of Jesus Christ given for all. How might Luke's genealogy challenge your current understanding of the elements if we regard all of humankind related by that blood to Christ and to one another?

Miracles should promote a *social memory*. Luke's genealogy accomplishes this task easily by asking the reader to remember the diverse history of the world—and the blood of Adam that courses through all our bodies. This genealogy demands that we recall our basic interrelatedness. If Jesus lives as our ancestor, we also live as kin to one another.

The fourth key (*talk about God*) raises

Why would God honor diversity over unity? Why must the life, death, and resurrection of Jesus hold worldwide implications (key four: God talk)?

Luke's Birth Narrative

Some of the comments here might challenge your current understanding of the birth of Jesus found in Luke. Feel free to refute, argue with, or even dismiss them. God speaks in many different ways through Scripture; this commentary only offers one.

Read Luke 2:1-5. Have a commentary on Luke on hand to check the record about what happened when and to check the factuality of Luke's report.

What does it mean to you to say that Luke's history is inaccurate, or is a conflation of historical data from a wider range of dates than just that of the birth narrative? Does this lessen the truth of what Luke has to say?

If these inaccuracies are deliberate by Luke in order to urge his readers to dig deeper, what can that mean for readers who do not understand this literary device?

important questions about the nature of God. Why would a God honor diversity over unity? Why must the life, death, and resurrection of Jesus hold worldwide implications? Can Jesus serve as both Messiah to the Jews while being the Savior to the entire world? Believe it or not, Luke explores these rather sticky questions throughout his Gospel.

Luke's Birth Narrative

Read carefully Luke 2:1-5. Notice the following statements:

• Caesar Augustus decrees all persons in the world should be registered.
• Caesar Augustus declares the census while Quirinius is governor of Syria.
• Bethlehem is called "the city of David."

Historically speaking, all three statements are false. First, no worldwide census was ever conducted by the Romans. Second, a Roman census (like the census of today) requires that citizens be counted at their current place of residence, not their hometown. Third, Quirinius's census of Judea most likely took place at least ten years after Jesus' birth. Fourth, while David was born in Bethlehem (1 Samuel 16:18), Jerusalem, which once was considered King David's own property, was thereby known as "the city of David." (See for instance 1 Kings 2:10, where David is buried in "the city of David," the capital of Jerusalem.)

Should such observations be considered blasphemy? heresy? Why would Luke's account be so different from the historical record? In short, because Luke knew that those who read his account would realize that those statements were false. How can this be?

In the ancient world, about five percent of

How, in our serious conversations, do we make comments or state ideas that are overtly false in order to communicate some truth? (Consider irony, understatement or exaggeration, or metaphor, for example.) How do you discern when to read (or listen) "between the lines"?

What role should history play in the study of Scripture? To what extent should the Bible be explored, using the tools of historical and literary research?

Visualize the Christmas cards and other Nativity art and songs that depict Jesus peacefully sleeping while the mangered animals seem to watch or even guard over him. How does it influence that vision to think that a farm animal might just as happily have taken a bite out of the baby?

How do you experience the world "devouring" Jesus and, later, the followers of Jesus?

the population could read; these persons usually held high social, educational, and financial status within their communities. They knew the history of their day, the names of rulers, the histories of the Jewish people. The statements that open Chapter 2 of Luke would have struck them as quite erroneous. But the ancient reader, being educated, would simply have taken these sentences to mean "the following statements should be read on a deeper level." Such a device—to use false statements to cue the reader to read the text symbolically—was used by many writers in the ancient world. Luke used a writing style of his time.

So, what is the "deeper level"? A worldwide event *was* about to occur and Luke did not mean the census. Mary gave birth to Jesus. And what did she do with her cloth-wrapped infant? Placed him in a manger, a feeding trough for animals (Luke 2:7).

Having worked a farm on various occasions throughout my life, I find this image of the baby Jesus in a trough horrifying. Mangered animals will literally eat anything placed in their trough. I know, because I took pride in placing all sorts of edible (and some inedible) items in the troughs. The animals always ate it. No exceptions. Some days, I would kick a trough. The animals would hear the sound of my foot striking the side of the manger and come running. Chow time.

Every Advent season, my local church dramatizes the Lukan version of the birth story, complete with a baby in the feeding trough. The woman portraying Mary looks down at the infant with loving eyes. The infant looks up at Mary, cooing. And I find myself thinking, "Gosh, I hope all the animals stay away, or that baby is a goner!"

Why would Luke tell this story? Because

If Jesus' destiny rested with suffering unto death so Christians might experience new life through his resurrection, then what is the destiny of the modern Christian? How might we live into that destiny on a daily basis?

he wanted the reader to understand the meaning beneath the event, in the same manner Luke wanted the reader to understand the meaning beneath the events that open the birth narrative. Mary placed her child in the manger because Jesus had come to be devoured by a hungry, sinful world. The manger became the penultimate statement of destiny. I often find myself wondering if the wood that gave form to the manger also gave shape to Jesus' cross. The first bed that Jesus' body touched—wood—was also the last.

Birth: A Miracle of Miracles ■

Review the miracle birth story by using the four keys. What does it mean to you to think that all births are sacred proclamations of God's historical presence in the world (key one)?

To what extent does our rejection of responsibility of the millions of children who die needlessly serve as a rejection of our connection with the Christ Child?

How does working for the benefit of any needy child (aftermath) testify that Jesus makes a difference in anyone's life? In the context of aftermath, how do you understand your role (and the presence of all other persons) in the body of Christ mentioned in 1 Corinthians 12:12-31? If the birth is a means to

Birth: A Miracle of Miracles

So, what relevance should the miraculous birth stories of Jesus, as told by Matthew and Luke, hold for the modern Christian? Again, the four keys provide a framework for investigation. First, we should strive to create a world in which all births become sacred proclamations of God's historical presence in the world. Sadly, millions of children around the world each year come to the world in conditions of abject poverty, disease, and malnutrition. To what extent does our rejection of responsibility for these infants serve as a rejection of our blood connection with them?

The aftermath of the miracle of Jesus' birth can be experienced in the rituals, beliefs, and actions that constitute our faith in a living Christ. Working for the well-being of all children, for instance, serves as testimony that the birth of Jesus still makes a tangible difference in our lives. So often we forget the words of Paul: we are called to be the body of Christ in the world (1 Corinthians 12:12-31). If Jesus' birth holds significance, it should call us to become his living body in a needy world.

The social memory of the birth of Jesus

social memory (key three) what effect does it have on your own family history? on communicating that history? on communicating your faith history and finding your place in it?

calls us to rehearse, retell, and reenact the history of God's people in the world. Sadly, many of us have become so self-focused, so self-absorbed, that we barely know the history of our own families. How much more important should it be to understand the history of God's people in the world? Intense study of Scripture, church history, doctrine, and world news establishes the necessary context for the miraculous births. When removed from its panoramic worldview, the effect of Jesus' miraculous birth loses its impact.

Jesus came to a broken world to offer hope; our own brokenness and need for hope stand as an infinitesimally small—but nevertheless important—dimension of this larger purpose. For the birth of Jesus to provide meaning and purpose to the world, we must become discerning students of the Bible. Christians have a vast, significant, and historically rich story of faith to share.

Finally, the wonderful birth of Jesus in specific raises questions about the work of God in all human life. To what degree could all births be declared "miracles"? Most persons who have experienced the birth of a child could attest to the glorious proclamation of God's hand at work during the event. But remember, the birth of children, to Christians at least, also brings the long-term effects of a miracle: the aftermath of a life changed forever by the presence of a child, the necessity to educate that child in the memory of the faithful, and the promise to raise the child in the context of a Christian family.

If God has designed all births to function as miracles in our world, how does God intend for us to accept responsibility for nurturing the result of those miracles—the children?

Miraculous births can render monumental responsibilities. If God has designed all births to function as miracles in our world, how does God intend us to live into the responsibilities and challenges of those miracles? And when responsibilities appear rejected or unfulfilled, who shall receive the blame?

The Church's Children

Baptism within the Christian church declares openly that the entire faith community holds responsibility for the miracle of every child brought into its midst. If a child matures in a manner that seems incompatible with Christian expectations, the church must be willing to take responsibility and offer itself as a loving, reconciling force for the child and his or her parents. Perhaps our culture's fascination with individualism and self-determination has undermined our willingness to accept such responsibilities. Instead, it seems easier to place blame upon the child, the parents, the media, schools, or other social institutions.

But if the miracle of the birth of Jesus possesses meaning for modern Christians, it must call us to the responsibility of living into the miracle of births, even if that responsibility seems to limit the sense of individualism that we have declared as a sacred privilege.

The Church's Children ■

Look at your denomination's practice of baptism. What promises does the congregation make on behalf of the person being baptized? How well have you accepted responsibility for these promises?

Closing Prayer ■

The miracle of the birth story unites all of us as kin to one another and to Christ. Take some time quietly to review your sense of unity with Christ and the children of God, then renew or make your commitment.

Form a circle around the table of baby pictures. Join in your circle prayer and close with this unison prayer: "God of the generations, you ask us to accept you as our heavenly parent. But, through the birth of your son, Jesus, you have laid upon us a second request: to accept the stranger as my brother or sister. Ever-present God, such a request scares us; the world seems so dangerous. Hold us in your arms, God, and help us be brave kinfolk to the world. Amen."

Session Three

Healing Miracles: A Prayer for Amanda

Session Focus ■

God heals a broken world in many ways. Christians are called to see the myriad ways God offers us wholeness through Christ Jesus. Even in death, we can remain one with God through Christ Jesus.

Session Objective ■

This session explores several of the healing miracles described in the Gospel of Mark for a deeper understanding of how God might work miracles in our lives today. The text also will encourage you to ask the question of divine justice: Why does God allow suffering in the world?

Session Preparation ■

Have available a commentary on the Gospel of Mark and study the passages mentioned in this session. Record insights concerning the social and historical elements mentioned by the commentaries concerning the healing stories. Look up the Web site suggested in the session for information concerning ancient medicine. To establish the theme of

"I am writing to you to ask for help."

The subject line of this recent e-mail captured my attention. When I clicked the appropriate box, the following message emerged on the computer screen: *"I am not sure how to start a prayer chain, but we need a miracle. Amanda, a six-year-old child of a close friend, has a massive malignant tumor in her back. It was discovered by her mother just a few weeks ago as they hugged one another 'Good night.' There has not been a good night in Amanda's house since. Doctors claim the cancer has spread throughout Amanda's entire body; no organ has been left undamaged. No known treatment in the world can help Amanda now. But maybe you can. Will you pray to God? Will you ask God to heal Amanda? Will you pray for a miracle? We all know God can heal this little angel, if it is God's will."*

A prayer for Amanda. What should I pray? What precedent do I have that my request of God to heal Amanda would actually make a difference? After reading the e-mail at least one dozen times, I decided to look to the Gospels of Jesus Christ for guidance.

Within this session, I invite you into a personal journey of faith, of sorts. My journey. My faith in Christ Jesus and my ongoing struggle to understand the miracles associated with Jesus as recorded by the writers of

healing throughout your meeting space, try some of these ideas:
• Bring pictures, books, and magazine and newspaper articles concerning healing, the modern medical profession, new medications, and advances in medical technology.
• Check your denomination's worship resources for a healing service. Ask your pastor to assist you in locating resources and in leading the service.

You will need a Bible dictionary for a "Bible 301" activity.

Choose from among these activities and discussion starters to plan your lesson.

Healing Miracles

If you have the proper license, open the session with a video clip from a recent movie or television series that addresses issues of sickness and health.

In what ways did you see God at work in the scene? If God was not viewed as present, what does that say about the presentation? about the participants?

Read the e-mail from Amanda's concerned friend. Compose individual or a group response to the e-mail. These letters can either be shared now or as part of a closing ritual.

the New Testament. We will explore the biblical precedents for healing miracles and the possibility that the Holy Spirit still promotes health and wellness among God's children. Finally, I will share with you my e-mail response to Amanda's concerned friend.

Healing in the Ancient World

In a time far removed from our own, the citizens of the Roman Empire knew nothing of bacteria, viral infections, cell mutations, antibiotics, sterilization, and contagious diseases. Instead, they knew what they saw: Persons often became sick, lost weight, and died. Sometimes their sickness would manifest sores, rashes, or other physical aliments that assisted doctors in relating the illness of one person to the illness of others. There seems to be a connection between the persons who were sick, but what phenomenon could account for such a strange occurrence? It would be literally hundreds of years before the invention of the microscope would introduce the world to the reality of viral and bacterial infections.

Within the Jewish community of Jerusalem, disease was thought to be a consequence of the believer's relationship with God. Something had gone amiss in the divine-personal dynamic; the relationship was "missing the mark" of true intimacy and connection. Identified as *sin*, this condition often invited evil spirits to invade the body of the believer. When such possession occurred, the believer would often fall ill, demonstrating numerous physical aliments.

Such ill persons would be presented to a rabbi. The rabbi was trained to recognize the symptoms of possession, diagnose the type of spirit involved, and prescribe specific behaviors and treatments that, historically speak-

Healing in the Ancient World

To what extent should Christian views concerning sickness dialogue with advances in medical technology?

How did the ancient biblical community understand the relationship of illness to faith? Is there any difference in this perception between the Old and New Testaments? Can you think of any reason God might inflict sickness, disease, or death on an individual?

Under what conditions might "sin" manifest physical abnormalities or illness?

Read Leviticus 13:9-17. Leprosy referred to any blistering, bubbling, or abnormality on the skin (anything from dandruff to cancer). The term also referred to mold, mildew, and imperfections in building materials. Leviticus promotes the idea that a pure God requires a pure people. In what ways does your life currently fall into the category "impure"? How might you be in need of healing?

Bible 301

Skim through the rest of Leviticus 11–15 for a better sense of what is in this "Doctor's Manual." Given how much more we know of science and medicine,

ing, had been successful in eradicating the sinful conditions and restoring the sick persons to an intimate relationship with God.

Glance at Leviticus 11–15. This collection of writings, composed during or after the Babylonian Exile (587–539 B.C.), served as an ancient "Doctor's Manual" for the rabbis of the ancient Jewish world. Identification and treatment of skin disorders, burns, birth, menstruation, hair loss, and body discharges made this document a fundamental read for ancient physicians. These chapters seemed to be written directly to the ancient physicians and not to a more generalized audience.

The "Doctor's Manual"

Notably, several "Doctor's Manuals" of the ancient Greco-Roman world have survived. To discover more information about medicine and medical practices during the time of Jesus, travel to this Web site, hosted by the University of Virginia: www.med.virginia.edu/hs-library/historical/antiqua/anthome.html

Jesus: Radical Healer in Mark

Keeping this critical background on the primary role of a rabbi as physician in mind, we turn our attention to the Gospel of Mark. Many healing narratives appear in Mark. Look at healing miracles that appear in the first chapter:

• Mark 1:21-27: Commands evil spirit to leave body of man
• Mark 1:29-31: Heals Simon's mother-in-law of a fever
• Mark 1:34: Heals many unnamed persons of unidentified illnesses and evil spirits
• Mark 1:40-44: Heals man of skin disease

what can we find as useful and faithful in these passages today?

Jesus: Radical Healer ■

Holy Jewish healers in the time of Jesus were often called *hasidim*. Many demonstrated the ability to perform miracles through prayer and acts of kindness. In what ways could Jesus be considered such a "holy man"? When did you last practice such "holiness"?

Form four groups to read aloud the healing miracles in Mark 1. What happens in each of these stories? How does Jesus function as a "holy man" in each of the stories?

Key One: Jesus Heals ■

Read Mark 1:40-45 and the other four "secrecy" references from Mark. Why, do you think, would Jesus want to keep his ability to work miracles a secret? How could such a secret be kept? (The neighbors might notice if you were blind, or lame, or dead yesterday, but today you are not!)

A nice sample of the many healing miracles is found in Mark: exorcism, curing women, and treatment of skin disorders. But Mark's Gospel does not simply want to chronicle these events; Mark also offers rich commentary on the healing powers of Jesus Christ. By using our four keys (historical perception, aftermath, social memory, talk about God), perhaps the motivations of Mark's telling of these sacred tales of wholeness will become evident.

Key One: Jesus Heals to Affirm the Promise of a Messiah

As a modern reader of Mark, our tendency would be to conclude that the healing miracles proclaim the power of the Holy Spirit working in the midst of the people. Of course, we would be correct, but only in part. The writer of this sacred story has another set of proclamations in mind. Read Mark 1:40-45 closely. After healing the leper, Jesus ordered him to "say nothing to anyone; but go, show yourself to the priest, and offer for your cleansing what Moses commanded" (1:44).

"What Moses Commanded"

The phrase "what Moses commanded" refers to the laws of purification found in Torah, the first five books of the Old Testament. In the case of lepers who were made whole, what did Torah demand? According to Leviticus 14:1-10, two birds and a few special plants for the purpose of blood sacrifice and purification, followed by a cleansing regimen of shaving and bathing. Jesus, like most Jews of the time, knew the necessity of blood sacrifice at the Temple in Jerusalem to promote purity among God's people.

Read Leviticus 14:1-10 to see the sacrificial and purification requirements for a healed "leper."

What might God require of modern Christians when they experience a renewal of health and wholeness? If Jesus should not be considered a savior solely because of his ability to heal the sick, why should Christians proclaim him as "Lord"? Find a copy of the doctrinal statements of your denomination (ask your pastor for assistance). Why do you accept Jesus as Lord and Savior?

But why does Jesus want to keep the healing a secret? Interestingly enough, Jesus' request of persons to remain quiet concerning their newfound health appears throughout Mark.

Read Mark 1:34, 5:43, 7:36, and 8:26. Each of these healing stories concludes with Jesus leveling the same request: Keep quiet. This "secrecy theme" only seems prominent in the healing stories found in Mark. But what could it mean? Perhaps it is Mark's way of telling the reader, "There is more to belief in Jesus as the Messiah than simply healing illness." By discounting the healing miracles in this manner, Mark proclaims that the work of Jesus will exceed the standard expectations of the Jewish community for a messiah. This Jesus must be proclaimed Lord and Savior, and not simply a healer (like Asklepios, mentioned in Session One) or an ancient prophet returned (like Elijah; see 1 Kings 17 to read of this prophet's call and earlier miracle work).

As modern readers of Mark, we should heed the author's warning. If we believe in Jesus *solely* because of his ability to heal the sick, perhaps we should reassess our relationship to him. Being the Savior of the universe seems to entail much more than performing the role of a divine doctor. While not intending to degrade the miracles of Jesus, the writer of Mark does press the reader to proclaim the Messiah as Lord and Savior based on a greater set of reasons.

Key Two: Disruption

Read Mark 2:1-12, a story of incredible disruptions. Destroyed roof. Bringing the sick in the midst of the healthy. Touching sick persons in public. Placing the other sacred healers out of

Key Two: Healing Disrupts the Medical Profession

Within the selected healing narratives of Mark, the reader notices that Jesus usurps the medical authority of the rabbis. Instead of telling the ill, "Go, present yourself to the priests and follow their instructions," Jesus

business. What are the key points in this story? How does the healing take place, and what is the reaction to it? What does this healing tell us about Jesus? about Jesus and his relationship to the religious and community leaders?

In what ways do we attempt to keep the healthy and the sick separated? How might this story challenge those attempts?

Jesus' healing actions could have challenged other healing institutions of Galilee to consider "downsizing" their operations. How has "downsizing" affected your life? The life of the organization that "downsized"? It seems that while such actions may promote the health of an organization, the same actions can be detrimental to others.

exercises the medical authority of the ancient healer. And his instant success at curing the sick and possessed effectively declared the time-honored Jewish profession of healing rabbi "out of business," at least while Jesus was present. No longer need the sick and infirm seek counsel with the healers of the ancient Temple; simply call upon Jesus and find health. By asking the *healed* (rather than sick) individuals to present themselves to the priests of the Temple, Jesus ensured that this message was heard loudly and clearly.

Read James 5:14-16. The writer of this letter realizes that the "old system" of Temple sacrifice and presentation of the sick to the trained rabbi has been replaced by a "newer" system of works performed in "the name of the Lord." But what about all the ancient medical personnel of the Temple? What about the thousands of persons who used the old system of healing? What about the persons whose livelihood depended on the operation of the "old medicine"?

Viewed in a historical-social context, the healings performed by Jesus would have generated incredible social disruption and religious turmoil. Imagine the numerous persons whose jobs, families, and religious faith would have been challenged by this freelance healer. Attached to no specific tradition or temple, Jesus offered the world access to an awesome power, free of charge. And such a "Give-Away" program of health and wellness would have been a severe threat to the medical profession of the time.

Modern Christians still find themselves standing in the "aftermath" of these ancient declarations. To what extent can the healing power of the Holy Spirit, made manifest by the actions of Jesus so many centuries ago, find

How might "wholeness" differ from a more concrete notion of "cured" or "no longer sick"? Do you see wholeness as a "sacred relationship between the human and divine"? Explain. What, do you think, is the role of the Holy Spirit in healing and wholeness?

a home within the actions and instruments of modern medicine? Must Amanda's family, for instance, declare the doctors and nurses who have worked with Amanda over the last several weeks incapable of managing both the institutions they represent and the faith that many of them profess? To what extent does the request for a miracle for Amanda suggest the spiritual bankruptcy of modern medicine?

Jesus' actions within the healing stories found in Mark suggest a radical shift in focus: a movement from understanding health as a commodity mediated by institutions (like temples or even hospitals) toward *experiencing wholeness as a sacred relationship between the human and the divine.*

These stories describe a new type of relationship between a broken person and a whole God. As a result, those ancient mediating institutions found themselves out of business. Perhaps modern medicine should take note of this proclamation of a social aftermath: Health care organizations that fail to promote the sacred relationship of wholeness may find themselves looking for new customers. When Christians feel broken, we often look for relationships of wholeness, using our relationship with Christ Jesus as the standard against which we measure all others.

Key Three: Larger Tasks ■

Read Mark 8:22-26. What did Jesus do to heal this man? (The Greco-Roman world thought saliva had • healing power.) Does it seem strange that this healing "took two tries"? What might that suggest? Has there been a time in your life in which Christ seemed to work "in

Key Three: Healing Reminds Us of Larger Tasks

Read Mark 8:22-26, a healing narrative unique to this Gospel. A rather strange tale: It takes Jesus *two* tries to restore full sight to the blind man. How odd. Was the man's sinfulness so great that even Jesus could not remove it in one attempt? Probably not. So why does Mark tell of this healing in this two-phase manner?

Let's continue to read the Gospel account

stages"? Can miracles occur in "phases" rather than all at once? Explain. Read Mark 8:27-30. What is the significance of each of the persons mentioned in the disciples' "Who's Who"? It seems important to Mark to put this healing into the context of Israel's history. Why, do you think? To affirm Jesus as Messiah in this setting is also important to Mark. What impact does this identification have on the healing? on the disciples? on you? If that identification is important, why, do you suppose, did Jesus ask them not to tell?

Bible 301 ☐

Use a Bible dictionary to research the works of Elijah, John the Baptist, Amos, Hosea, and Jeremiah. How was Jesus like each one of these ancient leaders? Make a list.

Then look up the term Messiah. What characteristics did the Jewish community expect in a messiah? In what way did Jesus fulfill these expectations. What do you mean when you call Jesus "the Messiah"?

that follows for more clues. Read Mark 8:27-30. Immediately following the healing of the blind man, Jesus asks the disciples, "Who do people say that I am?" The responses sound like a "Who's Who" of ancient Israelite history: Elijah, the famous ninth-century B.C. healer of God; John the Baptist, a desert prophet who declared the necessity of repentance before the coming of a messiah (see Mark 1:4-8); and "one of the prophets," anybody from the social reformer Amos to the visionary Ezekiel. The miracle of Bethsaida had the effect of helping persons rehearse Jewish history. In fact, it seems important to the writer of Mark that the healing miracles of Jesus are seen in light of the long-standing history of God with the people of Israel. Somehow, the healings performed by Jesus complement that history while projecting a unique quality.

When Jesus asked the disciples, "But who do YOU say I am?" (emphasis added) Peter chimed in with "You are the Messiah," the one promised by the prophets of old. As in other places within the Gospel of Mark, the disciples are then told not to say anything about his "true" identity to anybody.

Read Mark 8:31-33. When Jesus told them the Son of Man (the person who is fully obedient to God's will, like the expected messiah) would be rejected and killed, Peter offered Jesus a strict reprimand (what we call in the South a "dressing down"). In response, Jesus "dressed down" Peter, calling him "Satan," an adversary to God's purposes.

Even with the rehearsal of sacred memory brought about by the healing of the blind man, Peter did not understand the full mission of Jesus: Jesus came to fulfill the hopes and expectations of the faithful while also suffering pain and death for the sake of those same

Read Mark 8:31-33. How would you describe the "big picture," the purpose behind the life, death, and resurrection of Jesus? How do the miracle stories help you get the "big picture"?

hopes. While Peter saw the "big picture"—much like the blind man whose initial sightedness allowed him to see the outlines of people (Mark 8:24)—he did not understand the whole picture: Suffering and death play an important role in creating the kingdom of God.

Remembering Jesus only as a miracle worker oversimplifies the nature of the Christ, whom Christians declare as Lord and Savior. It is only through the suffering, death, and resurrection of Jesus—not the miracles—that new life in Christ becomes possible for us (see Romans 6:5-14). Miracle stories require that we keep this larger perspective in our minds and hearts, lest we reject or accept Jesus on the basis of miracles alone and throw into question the entire notion of Christian salvation through the cross.

But it becomes difficult to keep the "whole picture" in mind when we encounter such suffering and evil in the world. Why must a wonderful six-year-old child like Amanda die? How can God allow innocent persons to suffer? If Christians believe in the saving power of Christ because of the victory at the cross, then what role should healing miracles play in our daily faith? Is it wrong to ask God to heal Amanda?

Key Four: God and Evil ■

Exorcisms served as testimonies of God's struggle with demonic forces. Read the healing of the possessed man in the synagogue (Mark 1:21-28), the epileptic boy (Matthew 17:14-21) or the Gerasene demoniac (Luke 8:26-39).

Key Four: Healing Miracles Reveal God's Struggle With Evil

Within the Gospel texts, the healing stories depict Jesus as the one who can forgive sins and conduct battle with evil spirits. People made whole by the actions of Jesus experience the power God commands over evil in the world. But these stories of healing, for the ancient and for modern readers, are a small version of a larger, cosmic tale of the battle between the forces of good and evil. As humans, we are limited in our ability to

Exorcism comes from a Greek word meaning "to cause another to swear an oath." What "oath" should Christians take against evil in the world? How might this oath be demonstrated throughout our work with others?

How did Jesus overcome the dark spirit? How did the witnesses respond? What is the role of faith and healing? Is "faith" something quantifiable so that when you get enough of it you can do certain things, such as healing? Explain.

What aftermath is indicated in the story? Add your own "next chapter" (not necessarily an ending) to the healing story, based on where it seems to be going. What do these stories, and your addition, say about the presence and effect of evil in the world?

God's "Big Picture"

When have you last experienced "pain fatigue"? How does this condition affect your faith? Under what conditions might one make an "idol" of his or her own pain or suffering?

comprehend the massive dimensions of God's struggle with the forces of darkness. Healing stories give us a glimpse—on a very small, accessible level—of what God is attempting to accomplish on the universal scale: the total eradication of evil.

And Christian faith asks, based in the biblical witness, that we trust in God's ability to ultimately overcome evil and establish a final realm of peace and justice (Revelation 21). Meanwhile, evil continues its work in the world. Humans can be hurt, suffer, and die. Disease, often in a nondiscriminating fashion, can attack any member of the human family. Humans even remain capable of inflicting pain and suffering upon one another, sometimes on grandiose and grotesque scales, such as the Holocaust of World War II or the Rwandan massacres of the early 1990's. Given these events, it is easy to lose sight of God's ongoing work on the problem of evil.

God's "Big Picture"

Perhaps our requests of God for healing reflect our limitations in understanding the big picture of God's work against evil and our ever-growing sense of *pain fatigue*, the weariness, exhaustion, and depression one can feel when life becomes saturated with death, destruction, and tragedy. Think about the pain experienced by Jairus, a father whose twelve-year-old daughter died (Mark 5:21-24, 35). Jairus's anguish finds a contemporary expression in the lives of the parents and friends of Amanda. Totally dispirited, parents of terminally ill children turn to any known source of strength, solace, and solution.

Like Amanda's friend, Jairus turned to Jesus for assistance. And the daughter of this

In small groups, discuss the nature and origin of evil. What is "evil"? Should illness be seen as a sign of evil in the world? in the life of an individual? From where does evil originate? What purpose does evil serve in the world?

desperate father experienced new life (Mark 5:36-43). Why should Jesus accept the pleas of this ancient parent but fail to answer the cries of a modern family? Keeping in mind the "big picture" of God, addressing evil can be difficult in these highly personal, often publicized tragedies. But the death and resurrection of Jesus reminds me that God remains at work on the "big picture," even if the human condition limits my ability to focus on anything other than the particular illness of Amanda or of anybody else whom I might love who suffers disease and loss of life. My spiritual nearsightedness could lead me to erroneous theological assumptions, such as valuing my own pain over the pain of countless other human beings who suffer.

Although it hurts to admit, modern Christians can often make idols of their own suffering, using their own situations as ultimate litmus tests for God's presence in the world. "Take care of this one situation and I will believe you are working on the 'big picture,'" we find ourselves shouting. Like Peter, we must focus on the big picture of Christ, even when it is only one aspect—like Jesus, the miracle worker—we find ourselves craving more than anything else in the world.

Healing Miracles ■

On a piece of poster paper, write the four major ideas:
1. Christian life teems with miracles.
2. We hold responsibility for advancing the healing presence of the Holy Spirit.
3. Christian healing is best understood as a sacred relationship of wholeness between the human and the divine.
4. Our bodies are always

Healing Miracles in the Modern World

So what of Amanda? Should the family expect a miracle from God? After studying the Scriptures and spending several hours in prayer, I have arrived at the following conclusions. First, the Christian life teems with miracles. Parents give birth, persons find happiness, and many people live long and productive lives. Working through medical technology and technicians, the Holy Spirit advances blessings of wholeness upon the multitudes.

susceptible to injury, disease, and death.

Where do you find miracles? Do you think there is any such thing?

How can a person advance the presence of the Holy Spirit? What does that mean? If miracles are not rewards, but available to everyone, how do you reconcile that some persons experience them and others don't?

How would you define what is a sacred relationship of wholeness between the human and the divine? What difference can you find between "healing" and "wholeness"? What does submission have to do with healing and wholeness? What does it mean to you that God is aware of the suffering of each and every individual? Given that some persons suffer unspeakable suffering and evil, could it be that God was busy concentrating on the "big picture" and did not intervene for them?

Second, we hold an awesome responsibility for advancing the healing presence of the Holy Spirit within the world through the proclamation of Jesus' life, death, and resurrection and the sharing of medical technology and resources with all persons around the globe. As the miracle narratives in Mark suggest, healing miracles require that we share the good news will all persons, regardless of differences. Miracles of wholeness are not gifts granted to those "VIP Christians" who have followed all the rules, since gifts, by definition, come with no strings attached. Neither should such miracles be understood as a part of a mysterious reward system, since most folks would find themselves wondering why God had passed them by.

Instead, Christian faith tells us that *miracles of wholeness* can be understood as divine declarations of the wondrous work of God throughout the universe. Whenever somebody accepts Christ as a personal Lord and Savior, a healing has occurred. Whenever we find ourselves recommitting ourselves to the call of our baptism, healing happens. Whenever the Holy Spirit works through others to bring health, we find newness.

Third, Christian healing is best understood as the establishment of the sacred relationship of wholeness between the human and the divine. To be whole in Christ, we must submit ourselves to God, who needs our assistance in accomplishing the "big picture": the eradication of evil in the universe. Healing miracles remind us to hold hope in the "big picture," even when the "small picture" of our immediate lives appears dismal or hopeless.

Fourth, this human shell we identify as a body remains susceptible to injury, disease, and death. While God does not will specific events of illness or death, God remains keenly aware of our suffering as humans. And while God can do all things, God's focus remains on the ultimate goal: the eradication of evil in the universe and the creation of the New Jerusalem. God realizes that much of the "small picture" of human suffering rests within our power to diminish or even end it. Hatred, jealousy, and anger breed contempt for one another. It stands within our power as Christians to create a model of heaven on earth, a radical realm of peace and justice. Our willingness to seize responsibility for performing these small miracles of wholeness must bring joy to the heart of God; we are doing our part to eradicate evil in the world.

The Big and Small Pictures

God promises those who love God and one another entrance into this eternal realm of peace and justice, Heaven. For this reason, many Christians keep their eyes set on the "big picture" of God rather than the "small picture" of human suffering. While such a shift in perspective does not take away the immediacy of the pain or loss, the promise of resurrection in Christ (1 Thessalonians 4:13-18) tells us that life does not end with death but that we are transformed by the Holy Spirit. Even when disease and death diminish our numbers, it cannot deplete our truth in the "big picture" nor our resolve to continue our efforts toward ending human suffering.

A Prayer for Amanda

So, what of Amanda? What words of comfort could I share with the concerned friend of the family? What prayer could I utter that would touch the heart of God? I sent the following e-mail as my response: "*Remembering Amanda has been part of my life for quite some time. I remember, for instance, when her mother*

How can the "big picture" be comforting or meaningful to someone, for example, who has been tortured and mutilated in the conflicts in Africa or paralyzed in a drive-by shooting in a US neighborhood?

The Big and Small Pictures ■

To what extent should Christians expect God to focus on the "small picture" of personal or human suffering?

Take a few moments to pray and reflect on your understanding of healing and miracles in today's world.

A Prayer for Amanda ■

If you did not already do so, share your e-mail messages that you wrote as if to Amanda.

Think about others you know (or yourself) who face devastating disease, trauma, or emergency. How does it feel to think that only a miracle would change the situation? Where do you look for hope? How do you hold out hope for others? How is hope to be distinguished from a refusal to assess a situation realistically? What role does prayer and faith in the Holy Spirit play?

Closing Prayer ■

God's healing presence is available to all, even if the miracle doesn't happen. Take time to reflect on how you perceive God's presence in your life, and then in prayer make or renew your covenant with Jesus Christ.

Join in your circle prayer and include prayers for all the Amandas of the world.

announced, 'I'm pregnant!' I recall the joy surrounding the birth six years ago, the pictures of the first step, and the stories concerning her childlike antics and adventures. Now the doctors inform us of Amanda's terminal illness. Remembering Amanda becomes evermore critical at this point.

"The life of Amanda reminds me that God has always remembered Amanda as well. There has never been a time when I failed to sense the joy of the Holy Spirit finding expression through Amanda's face, hands, and actions. God remembers Amanda, even during this illness. And the gospel of Jesus Christ declares that God will remember Amanda forever. Should cancer end her days with us, I will remember God's promise to hold Amanda in God's arms as her heavenly parent. While this idea does not stop the empty arms of Amanda's parents from aching, it does provide them something on which to hold instead. And should Amanda's condition improve, I will celebrate the power of the Holy Spirit to reinforce my belief in its continued work in the world to eradicate evil.

"So, I offer this prayer for Amanda: God, eternal parent of Amanda, your children are hurting today. Our humanness inhibits our ability to focus on the bigger picture of your work; our personal pain and grief masks our eyes from seeing your face. Grant us clear vision, even in the midst of our sadness. Help us see you standing with Amanda, holding her hand and calling her by name all the days of her life. And when the time comes for the sun to set on this young life, may I be blessed enough to view you embracing her soul and carrying her to the paradise promised all of your children. Amen."

Session Four

Perfect Deeds: The Seven Miracles in John

Session Focus ■

All persons can accept the gift of immortality offered by Jesus. Once received, this gift will bring significant changes to the life of the recipient. Perhaps this shift in focus, from worldly concerns to universal ones, constitutes the greatest miracle available to the Christian.

Session Objective ■

This session will explore the miracle stories unique to the Gospel of John. Using modern biblical scholarship, we will unpack John's message for both ancient and modern Christians. How can we partake of the gift of eternal life? What difference should it make in our daily walk with God?

Session Preparation ■

Looking at Session One, write the "Four Keys" on a large sheet of construction paper. Display this paper in a prominent location for in-class reference.

Find a dictionary of Christian theology or a Bible dictionary. Look up

Browsing the shelves of local bookstore, I found the "Self-Help" section stocked with dozens of texts concerning miracles. Some of the authors promise to share with the reader "secret knowledge" concerning the nature of miracles in the world. One writer offers the reader access to immortality and an ageless life. I could even access the secrets of the universe, as described by a three-thousand-year-old spirit, conveniently "channeled" by the author of another best-selling book. Choices, choices, choices.

As a Christian, I tend to reject the promises made by such literature on two grounds. First, such declarations of secret knowledge and channeled spirits seem irrational to me. The truth of the universe should be accessible to all reasonable persons. Second, my belief in Jesus as the Messiah makes other pathways for miracles unnecessary. While I am sure many persons find comfort from reading these miracle-oriented self-help books, I find the claims presented by the authors invite me to displace the authority of Christ with a belief in some other higher power or entity, a switch I am unwilling to make. Challenging divine authority by offering miracles and secrets to the masses has occurred throughout the history of the

the following terms: *Logos,
immortality, grace, incarnation, creation, atonement,
shalom*. Post these terms,
with appropriate defini-
tions, around the room.

Have on hand a Bible
atlas. "Bible 301" activities call for a Bible
commentary and a Bible
dictionary.

**Choose from among these
activities and discussion
starters to plan your lesson.**

Perfect Deeds ■

What is your understanding
of "eternal life"? How is
your understanding of
immortality informed by
the words posted within
the room?

Describe specific claims
made by recent popular
publications you see
regarding spirituality, healing, and miracles. How do
you engage such literature?
How do you think others
should engage this
literature? Why?

Lucky Number ■
Seven

Identify the possible current cultural or religious
meaning behind the following numbers: 3, 4, 7, 12,
13, 16, 18, 21, 40, and
65. How do you use these
numbers to convey deeper
ethical, moral, or social
understandings?

Christian church. In this session, we will
explore the Gospel of John as an early
response to such challenges, noting how the
writer describes the miracles of Jesus as an
ultimate proclamation of his authority as
Logos, or Divine Reason (John 1). As in previous sessions, we shall also use our "four
keys" to unpack these miracle narratives and
their possible meaning for our Christian
journey.

Lucky Number Seven

The miracle stories in the Gospel of John
differ from those recorded by the other New
Testament Gospels in several significant
ways. First, John only includes seven miracles, all of which occur within the first eleven
chapters of the Gospel. (Those marked with
an asterisk [*] appear only in John, and they
will be the focus of this session.)

• John 2:1-11*: Turning water into wine
• John 4:46-54: Healing the Capernaum offi-
  cial's son
• John 5:2-9*: Healing the paralytic by the
  pool of Bethzatha
• John 6:1-14: Feeding the five thousand
• John 6:16-21: Walking on water
• John 9:1-12*: Healing the man born blind
• John 11:1-44*: Raising Lazarus from the
  dead

These seven miracles seem to occur over a
two- or three-year period, since John mentions three different Passover celebrations
(2:13, 6:4, and 11:55). And, while John
admits that "Jesus did many other signs in
the presence of his disciples, which are not
written in this book" (20:30-31), he omits
those wonderful acts from his sacred story of
Jesus. So why settle on seven miracles? Why
not ten or twelve? Why focus on these par-

What does it mean to associate perfection and com-
pletion with the acts of
Jesus? In what way does
Jesus call you
to perfection?

Why, do you think, does
John omit so many other
miracle stories? You may
wish to consult a commen-
tary on the Gospel of John
for additional insights.

ticular miracles? Why does the writer stop telling miracle stories by Chapter 12? So many questions.

First, John assumes that ancient and modern readers will recognize *seven* as an intentionally selected number. Throughout the Jewish world, the number seven represented the concepts of completion and perfection. By limiting this account of Jesus to seven miracles, the writer conveys to the reader the idea that Jesus came to earth to reveal the perfect truth about God. For this numerical interpretation to be accurate, each of the seven miracle narratives found in John should tell the reader something of the divine mission and authority of Christ.

Second, most modern biblical scholars assume that the writer of the Gospel of John composed this record as a radical retelling of the life of Jesus, suggesting to the reader the eternal and divine nature of the Christ. Each of the miracle narratives composed by John points toward the divine dimension of the universal Savior, Jesus, offering the reader some unique and critical insight into his character.

Third, the seven miracles highlight what the writer of John *fails* to declare about Jesus through the use of miracle stories. For instance, John does *not* describe Jesus as casting out demons. Nor does he describe Jesus' miraculous birth (Matthew 1:18-25 and Luke 1:26–2:40) or transfiguration on a mountaintop (see Mark 9:2-8; Matthew 17:1-8; Luke 9:28-36). In this Gospel, Jesus does not institute the Lord's Supper (Mark 14:12-25; Matthew 26:17-30; Luke 22:7-23) or pray in the Garden of Gethsemane (Mark 14:32-42; Matthew 26:36-46; Luke 22:40-46).

Four of the seven miracles appear exclusively in John; only three hold parallels in the other Gospels. As a result, the keen reader will notice that the writer of John has a specific set of ideas concerning divine miracles and their role within the Christian community. By using our four keys to analyze the four miracles unique to the Gospel of John, we can discern these biblical insights concerning the wonders found in this unique story.

Water to Wine: Truth on Tap in John

Read John 2:1-12, the wedding feast at Cana. At the urging of his mother, Jesus creates 120 to 180 gallons (on another scale, between 600 and 900 fifths) of good wine from water that had been originally designated for Jewish purification rituals. While a few persons might be tempted to embrace this initial miracle tale found in John as biblical support for the consumption of alcoholic beverages ("If it was good enough for Jesus, it's good enough for me"), they would be missing the radical message of the story. This miracle finds Jesus functioning as a *creator*, a function expressly reserved for God the Father. And, although Mary encouraged Jesus into action, the Messiah offered the new wine as a gift to the wedding party, no strings attached. No promises to keep. No bill to pay. No laws to follow. Just enjoy the new wine. Only God, made manifest in the flesh, could perform such a creative act on such a massive scale. Let the party begin!

What is the nature of the party in Cana? The wedding feast serves as the excuse. What John wishes to celebrate appears much more profound: God has become flesh and now dwells among humans (John 1:14). This miracle makes the historic proclamation of the incarnation of God (Key One).

The events of Cana also declare that the work of divine creativity remains in process;

What is your denomination's understanding of the use of alcohol and the Christian life? Must persons abstain from all mood-altering substances if they proclaim themselves to be Christians? to be born again? What does it mean to you that Jesus (and everyone else) drank wine and used it at celebrative events?

Read John 2:1-12. What are the features of this story: who is at the wedding, where is it, what is everyone doing, what are the expectations of what should happen at this event, who interacts with whom and to what purpose and result, and so on (historical perception, Key One; aftermath, Key Two)?

What does it mean to acknowledge Jesus as a "Creator"? What does his transforming miracle call to mind (social memory, Key Three)?

The miracle at Cana suggests that God's creative work continues in the world. How have you experienced recently the creative force of God in your life?

God has not yet completed fashioning the world. While many persons—both ancient and modern—might have assumed the Creator's work complete with the onset of the world, John declares a radical description of a God who has not yet finished with the world. There seems to be one remaining task: to offer "grace and truth" to the world through an incarnation of God (Key Four).

"Who Wrote John?"

Many modern biblical scholars find evidence in the Gospel of John that the writer used three separate sources in the compilation of his sacred story. Chapters 1–12, often identified with the "Signs Source" material, provided the writer with the unique set of "sign and wonder," or miracle, narratives. A second collection of speeches attributed to Jesus, unique to the Gospel of John (see Chapters 14–17, for example) but different in writing style from other parts of the text, have been identified as the "Discourse Sources." The "Passion Sources," used in the fashioning of Chapters 18–20, hold strong resemblance to the Gospel of Mark; many scholars assume the writer of John possessed a copy of Mark's account of Jesus.

Who was John, then? Probably a well-educated member of a Gentile church at the end of the first century (A.D. 95–97), possibly a disciple of the apostle, writing to a diverse group of Christians. Of course, such a conclusion seems hard to reconcile with the writer of Acts, who claims John, the son of Zebedee, was unable to read or write (see Acts 4:13).

Such an assertion of incarnation may not have surprised a Gentile (non-Jewish) audi-

How can Christians cele-
brate the Incarnation (literally, the "making flesh") of
God on a daily basis? When
has God last "become
flesh" in your life (Key
Four, "God Talk")?

How can we say yes to
God's gift of immortality?
How might acceptance of
this gift change our daily
lives?

What would it mean to live
your life as if each day
were a celebration?

ence as much as the playful creativity exhib-
ited by Jesus. The old ideas of following all
the laws of Torah, sacrificing to the gods, or
even adhering to social customs of Rome
had just become obsolete (Key Two).
Providing generous amounts of wine with no
strings attached operates as a symbol for *grace*
(the Greek word, *charis*, means an unmerited
gift). God takes human form to fulfill a
promise made to humankind throughout the
ages: salvation from death and a doorway to
eternal life (Key Three). Maybe the wine
miracle of Cana served as the announcement
party for God's ultimate generosity! For
Christians, the party has never stopped; the
wine of grace remains available to all who
will drink from the cup of Christ.

"Eternal Life: No Waiting"

*The Gospel of John uses miracles to suggest
the immediate availability of eternal life to
the believer. This approach differs significantly
from the works of Mark, Matthew, and especially Luke, who contend that eternal life will be
awarded to the faithful at the end of time. Like
the wine of Cana, immortality comes in unlim-
ited quantity for all humans who will imbibe it.
This idea becomes a common theme associated
with the miracle stories, perhaps offered in its
most grand form in the story of Lazarus (John
11:1-44).*

Healing
in Bethzatha ■

Use the Bible atlas or the
Internet to uncover information about Bethzatha
(also known as Bethsaida

Healing in Bethzatha:
Knocking Out the Competition

Read John 5:2-9. The bubbling, swirling
waters of Bethzatha, associated with healing
temples (or "porticoes") constructed by the

and Bethesda). Notice that it sits within the city gates. Think about the many types of people who came to those healing waters.

What role should hot baths, acupressure, massage, aromatherapy, chiropractic care, and other homeopathic approaches to medicine play in our lives?

Read John 5:2-9. What do we know about the man waiting at the waters? What is his situation? What is the nature of the exchange between the man and Jesus?

This man was an elder for his day and age and apparently had either never worked or had not worked for a long time. If he were well and expected to provide for himself (with no or few relatives—5:7), what might his life be like? In the aftermath of his healing, how would his life change?

Have you ever had a dramatic, life-changing experience? (Remember Nancy from Session One.) What was the aftermath of that change for you? If you had known before what you know now, would you want that change to have occurred? How might foreknowledge have affected the sick man's desire (or lack of desire) to have his

Romans, suggest a scene of pilgrimage: hundreds of ill persons traveling to the soothing waters, looking for a miracle. Bubbling water can promote similar hope for healing among many persons of the modern age. How many of us, after a long day of work and hassle, have submerged ourselves in a hot tub of water or a steaming shower? Or, how many persons have found themselves seeking the medicinal waters of a natural hot spring? Better yet, who has sought out the revered waters of Lourdes, France, thought responsible for healing numbers of persons throughout the years?

Perhaps Bethzatha, located in Jerusalem, functioned as the "Lourdes" of Judea. Nevertheless, John tells the reader that Jesus arrived on the scene and took notice of a older man, "who has been ill for thirty-eight years" (5:5). Given the average life expectancy of an adult male during the first century (24.7 years), this man had been sick longer than most men had lived. Why bother, Jesus? Of all the hundreds of invalids gathered at the pools, why pick this one? The man did not even ask for Jesus' assistance. Instead, Jesus approached the man and asked a simple (if not silly) question: "Do you want to be made well?"

John suggests that the man did not know Jesus prior to the healing (5:13). Little would have stopped that man from answering Jesus in a hateful or sarcastic tone, "No, the sound of bubbling water helps me sleep" or "No thanks, I've grown accustomed to how this skin disease brings out the color of my eyes." But, miraculously enough, the man responded to the stranger Jesus in a civil manner, suggesting the sick man lacked assistance.

So Jesus healed him. Notably, the man did not request healing from the stranger. This healing narrative contrasts significantly to

life change?
The elder at the pool of
Bethzatha experienced a
miracle from Jesus,
although Jesus was a
stranger to him. Can per-
sons receive a miracle from
God even if they do not
possess a relationship with
Jesus? Would it matter that
they attribute the miracle
to luck or fate or some-
thing other than God?
Explain.

the countless stories explored in Session
Three. In those stories, *everybody* knew Jesus
could heal. In fact, people came in droves,
seeking out this faith healer. In some ways,
the story of John 5:2-9 stands as another
example of the gift miracle demonstrated at
Cana. Viewed in this light, the healing at the
pool of Bethzatha reiterates the theological
point established earlier: Jesus comes as the
incarnation of God to offer the world the
gift of eternal life, which remains immediately available for all who will accept it.

This watery miracle goes one step farther:
*you may accept the gift even if you do not know
the giver.* In theological language, eternal life
becomes available to all persons—even those
who have yet to know Jesus.

By selecting the least likely candidate for
healing (an older, perhaps terminally ill
invalid), Jesus demonstrated that even the
most forgotten and outcast of the ancient
world could accept the gift being offered. I
often find myself reading this story in light
of modern attitudes concerning the aged.
While I would like to think society has
altered its prejudicial views of the elderly
since the time of Jesus, I fear little has
changed. The word of grace found in this
miracle story: nobody can be too old to
experience the gift of eternal life.

Jesus performed a miracle
for a man who was essen-
tially as good as dead, in
terms of age and health. Is
there any such thing as a
"wasted" miracle, do you
think? How do you under-
stand miracles when an
Amanda, for example,
(Session Three) does not
receive one, while this
elderly man did? Is "worth"
or "deserving" an issue in
miracles? Explain.

Finally, John's depiction of the miracle
worker Jesus debunks a modern notion of
earning a miracle. Instead, the Gospel of
John declares boldly that miracles operate as
unmerited gifts that require no prior purchase or obligation. You do not even need to
buy one of the many "self-help" books available at your local bookstore. And while
warm, whirling waters may woo weary workers, such experiences will not offer the gift of
immortality. Nor come free of charge.

Healing the Blind

Read John 9:1-12. Explore the idea of "working the works." What does this mean?

The man and his parents had a very different response to the healing, partly because it was done on the sabbath. The healed man saw it as an act of God to be praised; his parents were both pleased for him, we assume, but afraid for themselves. And the man was driven out of the synagogue (9:18-34). Is there ever an inappropriate time for a miracle? Is it possible that the aftermath will be worse than whatever was miraculously changed? Explain.

Bible 301 ☐

Read all of John 9. Use a Bible commentary to mine the richness of this complex event. How does Jesus take on the notion of sin, of religious authority, of abusing power (as in expulsion from the synagogue), of health and wholeness, and of his relationship to God? What do you know about Jesus, God, and wellness from this story?

Think about a recent event in your life or the life of your community that persons described as "miraculous." How might this experience serve as a "divine announcement"? Take a few moments to imagine yourself as the

Healing the Blind: Look at Me!

John 9:1-12 refutes another popular notion often associated with disease, illness, or infirmity. Rather than confirm the misconception that sin manifests itself in the world as illness, Jesus declared illness as an opportunity for God to "works the works," that is, to show God's presence in the world.

While the *Synoptic* writers (that is; Mark, Matthew, and Luke) strive to make this point within their Gospel accounts, John takes the question to the extreme: Should physical challenges with which one is born (in this case, blindness) be considered a manifestation of the sins of the parents? Unabashedly, Jesus responds, "No."

But what does it mean for God to "work the works"? In the case of John 9:1-12, the term refers to Jesus' ability to demonstrate his divine nature to the world. For John, miracles serve as an opportunity for Jesus to make his godly identity known. This idea differs greatly from the writer of Mark, for instance, who portrayed Jesus as attempting to keep his divine status a secret. (Read Mark 1:34, 5:43, 7:36, and 8:26.)

By extrapolating John's notion of miracles into the modern world, the Christian would conclude that every unexplainable event speaks more of the ever-present nature of a creating God than of the blessedness or destiny of the individual or individuals to whom the event occurs. Wonders and signs serve as God's advertisement to the world: "Hey, trust me! I still dwell among you."

In the next section, we discover how Jesus' final miracle, the raising of Lazarus, reiterates this concept of miracle as "divine advertisement" while pushing the reader to a deeper understanding of the ministry of the Messiah.

lead designer of an ad campaign for God. What slogans might you use? What means would you use to promote your idea? How does the concept of "evangelism" fit into your agenda?

Raising Lazarus ■

Review the ideas concerning miracles found in John. Try paraphrasing these ideas in your own words.

Read John 11:1-44 and complete the following sentences:

• The last time I felt most like Mary and Martha,

_____

• God weeps with me when

_____

• I am like Lazarus:

_____

What happened in this miracle? How do the four keys apply here? (How is the event perceived, what is the aftermath, how does it evoke social memory, how does it prompt us to view and to talk about God?)

John mentions that Jewish chief priests of the Jerusalem Temple wish to kill the resurrected Lazarus (John 12:10-11), apparently because too many persons were accepting Jesus as the Messiah. Have

Summary Miracle: The Raising of Lazarus

Remembering the key Johannine principles regarding miracles will assist us in engaging this final act of Jesus with clarity.

• The miracles of Jesus reveal the truth of his identity as the Logos, the Divine Reason of God.
• God comes to earth in the form of Jesus to continue the work of creation.
• The miracles demonstrate the immediate availability of the free gift of immortality to all persons who will receive it.
• Miracles say more about the nature of God than the persons to whom they occur.
• Other offers of health and immortality should be understood as false proclamations in light of God's gift to the world.

Keeping these ideas in mind, read John 11:1-44. Perhaps the most grand of all of John's recorded miracles, the raising of Lazarus provides evidence of the creative mission of God: to bring the gift of eternal life to a broken, mortal world. By intentionally staying away from Bethany for several days, waiting for Lazarus to die, Jesus set the stage for this incredible declaration of his divine authority and mission.

Further, this miracle repeats the idea expressed throughout the other miracles unique to the Gospel of John: immortality exists as an unmerited gift, immediately available from God through Jesus. No longer must one wait until the end of time (see 11:24); God promises to provide eternal life through Christ for all who will believe in God (11:25).

Two additional insights find expression within this final miracle narrative in John.

you ever experienced rejection, persecution, or threats because of your religious convictions? What was that experience? What did you do? Where was your source of hope and help?

Look at two additional insights: Jesus grieved for his friend, and Jesus' proclamation of his identity to assure and proclaim God's sovereignty. What does it mean to you in practical and spiritual terms that God knows your pain? Is that comforting? Does it help? Why? One answer to our grief is that God promises eternal life. What does that mean? What does it mean to you?

Bible 301 ☐

Look up the three "I AM" statements (6:35; 8:12; 10:11; and any others you wish) and Exodus 3:13-15. Use a Bible commentary or dictionary to read more about the significance of "I AM." How might this social memory have influenced Lazarus's family and friends? How does it influence you?

First, the sentence "Jesus began to weep" (11:35) offers the reader a glimpse into the depth of understanding God possesses for the human sense of loss and grief. Not immune from the emotions of humankind, when God takes the form of Jesus, God inherits the emotions of humankind. In short: God knows our pain. Even though those of us who believe in Jesus find comfort in the promise of eternal life, we still grieve when a loved one dies.

Three years ago, I buried my father in a small country cemetery in southern Louisiana. My mother had died several years prior from pancreatic cancer. After the service, I found myself standing alone at the graveside, absorbed in the grief concerning the loss of my father and the remembrance of a long-absent mother. And while I did find comfort in the knowledge that both parents had accepted the gift of immortality offered by God through Jesus Christ, my tears still tasted bitter and my sobs echoed deep.

What brought me a sense of solace, however, emerged as my heart took me to John's telling of the raising of Lazarus: Jesus wept for his departed friend. Even though Jesus knew Lazarus and he would see each other again, soon, Jesus wept. This notion of a weeping God, a God who stood beside me at that grave, tearful and sobbing like me, offered an image of family that shall never be extinguished from my soul.

The second insight found in the raising of Lazarus rests in use of the "I am" statement by Jesus: "I am the resurrection and the life" (11:25) Within the Gospel of John, Jesus refers to himself with an "I am" statement on at least fifteen occasions. "I am the bread of life" (6:35), "I am the light of the world" (8:12), and "I am the good shepherd" (10:11) serve as only three examples. Unique to this Gospel, the writer seems to be making a point. What could it be?

Read Exodus 3:13-15. Most English translations rendered the proper name for God as "I AM." Perhaps John wants to remind the reader that Jesus exists as the penultimate manifestation of God. And, just like the burning bush to Moses, Jesus calls all persons to the prophetic task of delivering the world from sin and death by offering the free gift of eternal life.

Encountering Jesus ■

Read John 4:7-30. List at least twelve words or phrases that describe the woman at Jacob's well. Has there ever been a time that you were so involved in your own struggles that you failed to recognize Jesus?

Spend a few minutes writing a mock obituary for yourself. How will you be remembered by others? In what specific ways could the assurance of immortality liberate your lifestyle?

Read Deuteronomy 30:15-20. What does it mean to you to "choose life"? How does an understanding of God's work in miracles and in other avenues of human existence expand your notion of "life" and what life to choose?

Spend a few moments describing your image of shalom, or deep blessing. How can you assist others in finding the lifestyle of shalom?

Encountering Jesus Today

Sometimes I find myself feeling like the woman at Jacob's well who encountered Jesus. (See John 4.) Rather than spending my days hauling water, however, my time seems occupied by concerns of mortgage payments, car notes, credit card bills, clothing purchases, trips to the grocer, and work. While my tombstone shall certainly not read, "He died debt-free," I do find myself pondering the meaning and significance of all of this toil. How shall I be remembered?

Maybe the members of John's early Christian community struggled with the same question. Shall we be remembered by our ability to manage effectively the concerns of this world? By exploring John's understanding of the miracles of Jesus, I sense these early followers of the Christ received a special set of instructions: Accept the gift of immortality and spend the rest of your life loving God and one another.

Read Deuteronomy 30:15-20. Choosing the gift of life offered by God led the people of Moses to the experience of deep blessing, or what our Jewish sisters and brothers describe as *shalom*. This gift of life, however, requires the people of Moses to follow numerous laws and ordinances, known as Torah. Through Jesus, God offered the world a second opportunity for shalom. While not negating the viability and meaning of the law of Moses, God's gift through Jesus functions as an immediate pathway to immortality. No waiting. No credit check. No strings attached. And such freedom from the law of Moses should lead to a life of peace and justice, rather than worry and turmoil concerning one's ultimate judgment. At least, that was the idea expressed in John's Gospel.

Of course, bills must be paid, jobs must be engaged, and homes must be maintained. But need we base our worthiness as humans on such measurements? Accepting the gift of everlasting life provides the Christian a status that cannot be matched by any amount of money, any title, or any financial portfolio. For the writer of John, the greatest miracle the Christian can ever receive is available immediately, free of charge. Choose life and live in the spirit of Christ, sharing the love of God with all persons. Even the bill collectors.

Choosing life through Christ means you can pass by or be very discriminating about the "self-help" section of your bookstore; you have traded your anxieties of the world for the deep blessing of shalom. God loves you, stands with you, and shall never leave your side, even at death. No matter what. And while it may be healing to play with your inner child, important to search for hidden memories, and adventurous to try to sense your energies field, these experiences are secondary to the gift of eternal life offered by Christ.

Closing Prayer

The diverse miracles in John show us that God relates to us in both the most ordinary events and the most grievous. Take some time to reflect on how you see God in these extremes of life, and then in prayer make or renew your commitment to Jesus Christ.

Join in your circle prayer, then close with this prayer together: "God, you are the One who was when the world was not yet created. You are the One who has been ever since the world's creation. You dwell in this world, guiding our feet to the path of shalom. Grab our hands, God, and lead us through this world to the world yet to be. Amen"

Session Five

Feeding the Multitudes

Session Focus ■

This session raises two very important questions. First, what is the kingdom of God? Second, what role should Holy Communion play in the lives of believers in Christ Jesus?

Session Objective ■

The miracle of the feeding of the five thousand promotes fundamental values of the Christian faith. By taking notice of the similarities and differences among the various accounts of the miracle, the modern Christian will gain a rich appreciation for why the Holy Spirit led the Gospel writers to describe this central event in such unique ways.

Session Preparation ■

Incorporate into this session an exploration of Holy Communion from a variety of Christian traditions. You may choose to find a dictionary on Christian theology and look up the following terms: *Eucharist, communion, sacrament, transubstantiation, consubstantiation, remembrance,*

If retelling a story increases its impor-tance to a community, then the miracle story of the loaves and fishes must be con-sidered central to Christian faith. I remem-ber my fifth grade Sunday school teacher telling the miracle to the class, our pastor exhorting the virtues of sharing after read-ing the passage in church, and the leader of our church's Mission Society evoking the feeding of the five thousand as ample reason why our local parish should serve food at the homeless shelter. As I grew older, I came to realize this particular story is the only miracle of Jesus mentioned by all four Gospel writers. If all four Gospel writers described it, I reasoned, it must be true.

Being curious, I decided to read all *six* accounts (Mark and Matthew tell the story twice, with slight variations). While quite similar in style, these narratives also demonstrated notable differences. How could a Christian declare the similarities of these writings without also accounting for their unique qualities?

During this session, we will explore the five feeding miracles of the Gospels, using the four keys introduced in Session One. Perhaps accounting for the differences will lead to a deeper understanding of this wonderful sign from God, the intentions of each Gospel writer in describing Jesus, and a rich appreciation for why this miracle story remains central to the modern celebration of Christian faith.

Mark: Looking for a Few Good Disciples

Since most modern biblical scholars agree that Mark wrote his Gospel first (A.D. 65–70), let's start our study with his account. At first glance, however, we notice a unique problem: *which* feeding miracle account in Mark should we read? Read Mark 6:30-44 and Mark 8:1-10. Why would Mark include two stories of massive feeding? Did both really occur, or in the transmission of the oral and later written history was one story told twice? If there were two, why do the disciples in 8:1-10 seem surprised by the miracle, since Jesus had performed a similar miracle already? Time to break out our four keys and investigate this strange set of events.

Key One: Jesus as Elijah Returned

Most scholars assume Mark's original audience was a group of Jewish persons who declared Jesus an *apocalyptic messiah* (a son of God anointed by oil to bring about the end of time and reinstate Israel to its former glory as an independent nation of God). One of the signs for the end of time involved the return of Elijah, who had been taken to heaven in a whirlwind to live with God. (See 2 Kings 2:1-12.) How would faithful Jews recognize Elijah, since he ascended to heaven almost eight hundred years prior to the birth of Jesus? Simply, Elijah would reenact all the miracles that made him famous. Notice the interesting parallels established between the

Mark: Looking for Disciples ■

Remember the Four Keys: historical perception, aftermath, social memory, talk about God.

Compare Mark 6:30-44 with Mark 8:1-10. Keep in mind the similarities and differences as you work through the four keys.

Key One: Jesus and Elijah ■

Look up the word *apocalypse* in a general dictionary and in a Bible dictionary. What does it mean to say that Jesus held an "apocalyptic" view of the world? Can you think of any modern-day thinkers who could be identified as "apocalyptic"?

Using a Bible dictionary, look up *Elijah*. How central is this figure to Jewish faith? Look up the terms *Passover meal* and *Seder* in a Bible encyclopedia, or ask a local rabbi about the role Elijah plays in this sacred ritual.

Compare the parallels of Elijah in the First and Second Kings passages with Jesus in the Mark passages. If Mark actually thought Jesus to be "Elijah returned," then how was Jesus to overthrow the Romans? What does it mean to identify Jesus as a warrior? How would such a description of Jesus affect

actions of Elijah (and his protégé, Elisha) and Jesus of Nazareth (as depicted in Mark). Most modern scholars assume the parallel between the characterizations of Elijah and Jesus was more than mere coincidence.

- Elijah fled to the desert after a call from God (1 Kings 17:1-7).
- Jesus spent time in the desert after a call from God (Mark 1:9-13).
- Elijah raised a child from the dead (1 Kings 17:17-24).
- Jesus raised Jairus's daughter from the dead (Mark 5:21-24, 35-43).
- Elijah heard a voice naming his purpose (1 Kings 19:9-18).
- Jesus heard a voice that named him (Mark 1:11).
- Elijah's disciple Elisha left his family (1 Kings 19:19-21).
- Jesus' disciples left their families (Mark 1:16-20).
- Elijah miraculously fed with bread (2 Kings 4:42-44).
- Jesus miraculously fed with bread and fish (Mark 6:30-44; 8:1-10).

By using the stories of Elijah and Elisha as a model, the writer of Mark proclaims Jesus as Elijah returned: an apocalyptic messiah who would displace the Romans from Palestine and serve as king of a new Israel.

Does the idea that Mark used the miracles of Elijah and Elisha as templates for telling the life of Jesus suggest that Jesus never performed those wonderful acts of healing, feeding, and restoration? Absolutely not! Mark simply casts these incredible acts from the life of Jesus into a form of writing that would convey a deep historical and theological significance to his Jewish audience. Like Elijah,

your understanding of the word *disciple*?

Key Two: Jesus and Order ■

Skim over Mark 6:30-44 and underline or identify the different numbers of the story. Read also Mark 5:2-13 and keep *legion* in mind.

Decipher the use of numbers in the sayings below:
• Y2K
• "It's six of one and a half dozen of the other"
• "Two shakes of a lamb's tail"

Numbers in Mark 6 ■

How many "number sayings" can you recall? Write these on poster paper or a chalkboard. What purpose do these numbers serve? How might a person a thousand years in the future understand these sayings?

What is the significance of *legion*; the number of denarii mentioned; the number of baskets, fish, and loaves; and the number of people who ate?

Why would Jesus and the writer of Mark use numbers in this manner? What place does *symbolic language* hold in the development of Christian faith? How might symbolic language serve as a means by which to distinguish "insiders" from "outsiders"? Who are the

Jesus was about ending political and economic oppression while creating a peaceful kingdom of God.

Key Two: Jesus Disrupts the Social Order

Read Mark 6:30-44 slowly. Notice the numbers mentioned: *two hundred* denarii, *five* loaves, *two* fish, groups of *one hundred* and groups of *fifty*, *twelve* baskets left over, and *five thousand* men who ate. While modern readers often skip over the numbers, the ancient listener would have found these figures central to the miracle

Working the Numbers in Mark 6

Let's start with the largest number: *five thousand*. Does Mark refer to this number at another point in his Gospel? What affiliation might the original audience have attributed to the figure? Read Mark 5:2-13, an account of the exorcism of the man from the land of the Gerasenes. When Jesus asked the spirit, "What is your name," it replied, "My name is *Legion*; we are many" (italics added). The term "Legion" refers to the foot soldiers of the Roman army, who would travel in groupings of *four thousand to six thousand* men. By the way, most legions traveled in divisions of *fifty* and *one hundred*. The numbers *five thousand*, *one hundred*, and *fifty* would have been familiar ones to the original Jewish audience, who suffered through a major war with Rome as Mark wrote his Gospel account.

Two hundred denarii represented almost one year's worth of wages for a laborer. When the disciples asked Jesus, "Shall we go and buy two hundred denarii worth of bread?" they asked a double-edged question: "Shall we actually buy that much food" and "Shall we actually jeopardize our own sur-

"insiders" within your religious community? How can you tell?

How do you react to the disciples' double-edged question about buying so much bread? When the dimension is added that they are making (or possibly making) such a sacrifice for strangers, how does that affect your understanding of the situation and of the disciples' place in it?

If the interpretation of "five fish, five fingers . . ." implies that the crowd was being invited to build the Kingdom with God's help, what is the implication for us today?

How do you interpret and understand the possible political overtones in this feeding miracle? How does that affect your hearing of the miracle now, especially if you have only been taught that the "miracle" was centered in sharing and generosity?

Numbers in Mark 8 ▪

Read through the numbers in Mark 8:1-10. What does this new set of numbers add to the understanding of the event?

How do you understand Key One (historical perspective) and Key Two (aftermath) after investigat-

vival for the well-being of these strangers?"

Twelve is a number resonating with hope, joy, and familiarity for any Jew. This sacred number designates the number of the tribes of Israel who journeyed in the wilderness with Moses (see Numbers 1:1-54) to establish eventually the ancient nation of Israel. By having twelve baskets (and twelve disciples), Jesus declared the fulfillment of a great political and sacred promise: to regenerate the independent nation of Israel.

The numbers *five* and *two*, some scholars have suggested, represent the five books of Moses or Torah (Genesis, Exodus, Leviticus, Numbers, and Deuteronomy) and the works of Torah and the Prophets, two of the three divisions of the Hebrew Bible with which first-century Jews would have been familiar. Yet I have heard an equally compelling interpretation: five loaves, five fingers; two fish, two fists. A shorthand way of saying, "With God's help, we will build the kingdom of God with our own hands."

Reading through the numbers, the feeding miracle of Mark 6:30-44 offers a startling conclusion: Jesus was calling persons into an army-like group for the purpose of using their own hands, resources, and lives to overthrow the Romans and reestablish an independent Israel, representing all twelve tribes of Jacob.

Numbers in Mark 8

Now read Mark 8:1-10, taking notice of the numbers. The numerical figures from Mark 6:30-44 have disappeared. Instead we have *three* days, *seven* loaves, *seven* baskets, and *four thousand* people. The term "three days" appears in the Old Testament about forty times, often used as a general way of saying, "in the fullness of God's time." Most

ing what all these numbers could suggest?

When might a Christian need to resist a government or national authority?

Do a bit of research on the "Jewish War," using the Internet, Jewish history books, or an encyclopedia of the Bible. Thinking that Mark may have written his Gospel during the Jewish War with the Romans (A.D. 66–70), how might such extreme social conditions have influenced the author? the first readers?

Jewish communities understood *seven* as the sacred number of completion. And *four thousand* resonated with memories of Roman troops marching upon cities and villages. By performing the miracle a second time in a unique manner, Jesus promoted a similar message: "The time is fulfilled, and the kingdom of God has come near" (Mark 1:15).

But that Kingdom would only emerge through social disruption, political turmoil, and possible persecution and death. While the followers of Jesus feasted on fish and loaves, they found themselves instructed in the deeper truth of the movement: The time is now to rid ourselves of the Romans and build the kingdom of God. Let us band together and fight in the name of God for our Promised Land. Needless to say, the Romans would hardly have found this message—or the man who delivered it—appealing. Political insurrectionists would meet their untimely end on a cross. Was this to be the fate of Jesus, the apocalyptic prophet, and his followers?

Assessing the Risks

What would you be willing to risk to build the kingdom of God? What level of importance do you place on the values of justice, peace, and equality?

Can you think of instances in which you "consumed the truth of God while not completely understanding the truth"?

Assessing the Risks

Reading through the numbers, the radical political and social nature of the feeding miracles in Mark seems hard to reject. To what degree am I prepared to risk my career, social standing, and even life to promote the message that Christ comes to the world to show us how to construct the kingdom of God? How easy it seems for me to consume the miraculous feast of God's word, savor the sweetness of God's presence, yet refuse to sense the deep responsibility that comes from dining with Jesus.

Instead, ours is a generation of spiritual "fast food": offer shallow answers to deep questions with no responsibility to others required. Instant salvation: just add (baptismal) water. Like the disciples in Mark, so many of us have consumed the truth of God available through Jesus while not completely understanding that truth. Mark believed that Jesus wanted those persons who declared him Lord and Savior to begin the process of building the Kingdom, even in the face of political, economic, or social oppression.

John: Jesus as the Bread of Life

Holy Communion can promote both feelings of humility and awe. By participating in this sacrament, I also feel a sacred, historic solidarity with the billions of Christians throughout the ages who partook of the body and blood of Christ. In a literal manner, this action forges a holy connection between me and all persons who have ever followed Jesus and proclaimed him as Lord. For a brief moment, we exist in a mystic, timeless unity that words fail to express.

Ancient documents like the *Didache* (DID-uh-kee), an instruction manual written for Christians around A.D. 100, as well as the letters of Paul, advocate the centrality of the Lord's Supper to the early Christian community. Another writing composed a few years prior to the *Didache*, the Gospel of John, seems to reinforce the fundamental place *Eucharist* (from the Greek, "gratitude" or "thanksgiving") held within the Gentile (non-Jewish) churches.

"The Didache"

While virtually unknown until the late 1800's, the Didache *(DID-uh-kee, a Greek word meaning "Teaching") provides the reader a glimpse into the life of an early Christian*

John: Jesus, Bread of Life ■

Spend time describing your most memorable experience of Holy Communion. Recall the setting, words, participants, and feelings. In what specific ways did this experience of Eucharist differ from other occasions?

What training do prospective members receive within your denomination regarding the beliefs and rituals of your denomination? Find some of the literature used to teach prospective members about your tradition. What does this material say about Holy Communion? prayer? other aspects of the Christian life?

Invite participants to follow the suggestion found in the *Didache*: recite the Lord's Prayer three times a day. Agree to try this ancient spiritual discipline for one week. Discuss possible outcomes to this practice. Why, do you think, would this practice have been instituted by churches in A.D. 100?

community. Instructions concerning the practice of baptism, the Eucharist, fasting, and prayers offer modern Christians a sense of how the earlier followers of Jesus behaved. The Didache also contains a version of the Lord's Prayer that parallels the version found in Matthew (6:9-13) and should be recited three times a day.

Suggestions for dealing with traveling prophets and apostles also denote possible problems with conflicting messages and behaviors from such folks. You might find this document online by searching the key words, "Apostolic Fathers," a collection of writings from the early church leaders of which "The Didache" is a small part.

A Meal for Gentiles

Read John 6:1-15, noticing the differences between this version and Mark 6:30-44. John's account provides specific information not mentioned by Mark. First, John must tell the reader *which* body of water Jesus crossed, suggesting the original reader would not be familiar with the Sea of Galilee (but would apparently know its Romanized name, "Sea of Tiberias"). As a result, most scholars conclude that John penned his biography of Jesus for non-Jews living away from Palestine.

Second, John mentions disciples by name, especially Philip, for whom this entire event became a "test of faith" (John 6:6). Third, the miracle occurred on a mountain at Passover. In the ancient world, sacred events often occurred on mountaintops, due to their proximity with the heavens, the dwelling place of God. If John placed the miracle meal during Passover, John wished the reader to conclude that no Jews would be present

A Meal for Gentiles ■

Compare and contrast John 6:1-14 with Mark 6:30-44. Make a list of similarities and differences on a piece of poster paper or on the chalkboard. How do you account for the differences found between the narratives?

If this miraculous feeding took place during the Passover so that it could not have had Jewish participants, but only Gentiles, what impact does that possibility have on your understanding of the story? Does it matter who attended? Does it reveal something new to the crowd and to John's readers about Jesus? If so, what? What does it reveal about Jesus to you?

for this event, since they would be engaged in the ceremonies of their high holy days.

As a skilled storyteller, John recreated the scene of the event, describing the feeding of the five thousand as the first sacred gathering of Jesus with the Gentile community of Galilee. Instead of calling the people into an army-like configuration for the sake of causing conflict with Rome, Jesus used the opportunity to reveal himself as Lord and Savior of the world. The miracle simply affirms this assumption. (Read John 6:14.)

As we explored in Session Four, John uses miracle narratives to declare the true nature of Jesus and the immediate availability of eternal life for all persons who would believe. So when the Gentiles who partook of the miracle meal awakened the next day to discover that Jesus and the disciples had returned to Capernaum, they jumped in their boats to find him. But why did they seek Jesus? Were they simply hungry for another miracle? Jesus responded to the curious Gentiles, "You are looking for me, not because you saw signs, but because you ate your fill of the loaves" (6:26). Sadly, the poor Gentiles had yet to understand the true nature of what had happened the day before. Miracles only point to the truth of God and should not be sought as ends in themselves.

Key Three: ▪
Sacred Memory

How does Holy Communion "point" believers toward Jesus? Specifically, what truth concerning Jesus does the sacrament of Holy Communion attest?

Key Three: Miracles Call for the Rehearsal of Sacred Memory

John 6:27-34 shows Jesus and the followers exploring the central stories of faith from the Jewish tradition: Moses delivered God's people from bondage and provided them Torah, the Law of God. Using the story of God providing *manna* for the persons wandering in the wilderness (see Exodus 16:4, 15 and Numbers 11:7-9), Jesus reproached the

How do you deal with fears regarding death and dying? At what points do you find strength and comfort in your religious beliefs?

Read carefully the Scripture passages mentioned in this section. How did the miracle evoke the memory of the Jews' ancient history? What connections would they make? What new steps might they take other than simply remembering the past?

Spend a few moments thinking about what these miracle stories say about the nature of God. How does the grace of God, for instance, find expression in these miracles? How does your past experience of God enable you to see God at work in the present and hope for (and recognize) God's work in the future?

followers, telling them the law of Moses failed to represent the true manna. Instead, Jesus states, "I am the bread of life. Whoever comes to me will never be hungry" (John 6:35, 48). While not declaring the law of Moses ("the manna from the wilderness") bankrupt, Jesus claims such gifts did not offer their ancestors instant eternal life.

When somebody accepts the flesh of Jesus, surmised John, they receive the free gift of eternal life. For John, the celebration of the Eucharist (Holy Communion) provided the believer access to the promise of immortality offered by God through Jesus Christ, a promise declared throughout the Old Testament but made available for all through the crucifixion of Jesus. For this reason, even the most ancient of Eucharistic prayers reveals a necessity to rehearse the promises made to our Jewish and Christian ancestors regarding eternal life.

In short, John changes the feeding miracle into a symbol for the first Eucharist, the central event within the life of the church. Through John's eyes, my sense of communion finds even greater historical depth. Every time I partake of the elements, I share a sacred connection with those Gentile followers on the distant mountaintop so many centuries ago. Like them, I acknowledge Jesus as the bearer of immorality. By participating in this ancient sacrament, I also admit to the shallowness of my fear of death and destruction. Yes, this flesh shall fade away; but, through Christ Jesus, I shall live forever. Given such blessed assurance, I find the courage to attempt to heal the hurts of a broken world.

Compare Matthew 14:13-
21 with Mark 6:30-44.
The main difference is
Matthew's focus on healing
and Mark's focus on teaching. Using Key Four, think
about how these two sto-
ries portray God. What is
the reader encouraged to
learn about God and how
God interacts with
humankind? What do these
stories tell you about how
God can or does interact
with you, personally?

In some Christian tradi-
tions, one must be forgiven
of sin prior to receiving the
sacrament of Holy
Communion. What role do
confession, repentance,
and absolution play in your
faith? If necessary, find a
dictionary and look up the
meaning of these terms. In
your denomination, must
one be made "whole"
before receiving the body
and blood of Jesus?

How might participation in
Holy Communion resemble
a miracle? How might
those who partake of the
blessed sacrament become
"miracle workers"?

Matthew and Mark:
Pointing Toward God

A comparison of Matthew 14:13-21 with
Mark 6:30-44 illustrates numerous parallels
as well as differences. Most notably, in the
Matthew account, Jesus feels compassion for
the "great throng" and begins to *heal* them
(14:14). In Mark, however, Jesus provides
additional *instruction*; he "began to teach
them many things" (6:34). If Matthew borrowed this story from Mark (as many scholars suggest), how can we account for the differences? What is Matthew trying to tell his
audience regarding this miracle, specifically,
and perhaps about miracles in general?

In Mark's account, Jesus invites the disciples to travel with him to a resting place,
apparently due to the exhaustive work of
casting out demons and healing the sick
(Mark 6:13, 30-31). Neither the disciples nor
Jesus seems aware of the fate of John the
Baptizer, described in Mark 6:14-29.
Oblivious to the death of John, Jesus and
friends journeyed by boat to a nice, getaway
spot.

In Matthew's account, however, the disciples of John inform Jesus of their teacher's
death (Matthew 14:12). In response, Jesus
withdrew by boat to a lonely place. I cannot
help but feel compassion for Jesus at this
point. Imagine how the news struck to the
core of his heart. With the death of John the
Baptist (who was also his cousin), the rules
had changed. The promised Judging Messiah
(see Matthew 3:7-12) had to switch gears
from what Matthew indicates is a mainly
teaching ministry and start the work proclaimed by John. Let the judgment begin.

So for Matthew, the feeding of the five
thousand occurs in the midst of *healing*, persons being forgiven of their sins and made

whole through Jesus. Once healed, these persons could partake of the bounteous blessings available from God. While Matthew retains the general outline of the healing story from Mark, the writer's changes suggest a new purpose for the miracle. All who find forgiveness through Jesus will experience the fullness that comes with a relationship with God. As John the Baptist predicted, Jesus began to "gather his wheat into the granary"—those who receive wholeness of spirit from Christ—while allowing those who would deny such generosity to meet the fate of destruction (Matthew 3:12).

By taking the bread, the many persons healed by Jesus are transformed into his blessed "wheat," worthy of inclusion into God's perfect realm, the kingdom of God. At the God-led hand of Matthew, this miracle proclaims the richness of God's mercy and Christ's invitation to all persons to enter a new existence in Christ. To be gathered into the arms of Christ signifies one's "wholeness" or spiritual health.

Joining the Family of God ■

Read Luke 9:10-17. How does Luke seem to combine the story emphases of both Matthew and Mark? What difference does this make in the way you understand and appreciate the miracle? How does this "miracle mosaic" influence your understanding of God?

Read Luke 9:7-9. What do you recall about Herod from previous sessions or

Joining the Family of God

By using Key Four (miracles talk about God), we have shifted our focus from mere occurrences to rich purpose. For Matthew, the miracle of the feeding of the five thousand occurs so persons can understand that healing occurs before inclusion, or perhaps because of it. When one enters the family of God, one experiences a newness of life not available by any other method or means.

Luke's account of the feeding miracle (9:10-17) appears to mix the accounts of Matthew and Mark. Many biblical scholars assume Luke borrowed a copy of both to create a "miracle mosaic," a collage that advocates numerous reasons behind the per-

other studies? How does "placing him at the scene" (or really before the scene) color the significance of what Luke is writing?

formance of this miracle. As if to say, "Both Mark and Matthew are correct," Luke's version promotes the social disruption motif found in Mark *and* the inclusion theme of Matthew.

Read Luke 9:7-9. By placing the story of mean, nasty Herod looking for Jesus immediately before the story of the feeding of the five thousand, Luke tells his reader, "Rome thinks Jesus a major social revolutionary," actually enhancing the ideas expressed in Mark's version. Likewise, Luke includes Matthew's "healing the sick" element to promote the necessity of wholeness before entering the kingdom of God. And by placing the event in Bethsaida, a major Roman crossroads and center of Jewish learning during the life of Jesus, Luke tells his readers that Jesus' offer of salvation and eternal life is available to *both* Jews and Gentiles. By blending the best elements of both Mark and Matthew, the writer of Luke promotes his prominent theme of universal salvation.

Becoming the Crowd

Imagine that you were present for one of these miraculous feedings. How do you "become the miracle"? In what arenas do you see this or other miracles at work?

In what ways do you see the presence of God's kingdom?

Becoming the Miraculous Crowd

The feeding of the five thousand demonstrates how God's kingdom can shatter old behaviors and expectations of persons who believe in Jesus Christ. Whenever one works at a homeless shelter, listens to Sunday school teachers and pastors, reflects on Scripture, or responds to the needs of a stranger, this miracle occurs again. Can you sense the kingdom of God in your life and community?

Miracles happen as God's realm of justice takes shape. By living in this world as if the Kingdom has already arrived, you make miracles possible. You become the miracle. Offer

Christ to the world through your daily prayers and actions and watch the miraculous work of the Holy Spirit change lives and promote justice.

Closing Prayer ■

The Eucharist is a natural ritual in which to review your covenant with God because of its covenantal nature. Invite your pastor to lead participants through the sacrament of Holy Communion. Pay attention to the words spoken, actions taken, and promises made. Remember: you are participating in a historic action of the church universal, a sacrament that connects you to the believers of the first century as well as to Christians around the world. Take time during the prayers to make or to renew your commitment to Jesus Christ.

Close with your circle prayer, and offer a prayer concerning the mission and ministry of the church to the world. Ask for God's help in building the Kingdom through acts of peace and justice.

For Next Week ■

Bring in photos and other mementos of special women. See "Session Preparation," page 76.

Session Six

Miracles and Women

Session Focus ■

Jesus sought to dissolve oppression and bias among God's people. Worldwide, however, women continue to suffer injustice, abuse, and murder based on their gender. The miracle of the Resurrection calls Christians to eradicate the conditions of oppression in our hearts and world.

Session Objective ■

To explore the critical roles women played in the miracles of Jesus. Much of Christian literature has been unduly silent on this important message of justice. Women served as disciples and witnesses to the Resurrection. This session will promote the miracle of radical equality within Christian communities.

Session Preparation ■

Bring in photographs, books, poems, or other articles that celebrate or point to the women of faith in our lives, and your life, today. Place these materials around the room. You may also wish to write the names of famous women of the Bible and church on

"Soon afterwards [Jesus] went on through cities and villages. . . . The twelve were with him, as well as some women . . . : Mary, called Magdalene, . . . Joanna, . . . and Susanna, and many others [women], who provided for them out of their resources" (Luke 8:1-3).

"God of the Exodus, hear the cry of all Your suffering people, women who hunger, women who hurt, women who are despised. Long have we been in exile, cut off from our roots in the holy places because we are feminine. Lift the burden of gender and class and lead us into freedom, where all are one in spirit and truth" (*Woman Prayer, Woman Song: Resources for Ritual,* by Miriam Therese Winter. Oak Park, Illinois; © 1987 by Meyer-Stone Books; pages 143–44. Used by permission of The Crossroad Publishing Company).

While Azureti missed her friends and family whom she had left behind in Swaziland, Africa, her heart did not grieve the conditions under which she had lived. Impoverished, abandoned, and often abused, young women like Azureti were treated as less than second class citizens. Coming to live and study in the United States offered release from these conditions. Or so Azureti had hoped.

large index cards. Place these cards in various locations throughout the room.

Choose from among these activities and discussion starters to plan your session.

Miracles and Women

Open the session with a dramatic reading of the two introductory quotations on page 84. In prayer, invite God to help us hear the words of liberation and joy concerning women in the world.

OR: Pray together the prayer in "Women" on page 95. During the recitation of that prayer, ask a class member to ring a small bell or beat a drum every eight seconds. Every seventeen minutes during the session ask another class member to blow a trumpet, sound a chime, or drape part of the altar table with black felt. Of course, inform participants of the use of these dramatic elements prior to the start of the session.

Invite a participant to read aloud the first two paragraphs of the story of Azureti. Where have you heard a story like this before? On poster paper or the chalkboard, list key words, ideas and "image words" from the responses.

Form groups of two or three persons. Ask each

Sadly, over the last three months, Azureti has faced numerous encounters of racial hatred, prejudice, and oppressive treatment of women. A tearful Azureti spoke to me recently of her shattered hopes for the United States to be "a better place, like Moses' land of milk and honey. But much of the milk tastes sour to me, and I find myself receiving more stings than sweetness from the bees of your people." Rather than resignation, however, Azureti believed that her faith in Christ Jesus could turn around both the actions of the oppressors and the lives of those who suffer.

To offer biblical support to her conviction, Azureti showed me several passages in the Bible that declared God's special relationship with women and the radical transformation possible for both oppressed and oppressor through Christ. While I had studied these passages on many prior occasions, reading them in light of Azureti's life offered me a new level of richness, compassion, and recognition.

In this session, we will explore the special role women played in the miracles of Jesus. While most of our work will be concentrated in the Gospel of Luke, the insights and questions raised within this session should be applicable throughout the biblical witness. Did Jesus' miracles affect women differently than men? What type of social disturbances might have Jesus' miracles involving women caused? And what specific statements do these miracle stories make concerning the nature of God, gender, sexuality, class, and the kingdom of God? Using our "Four Keys" we might stumble on some rather unexpected surprises.

group to complete the following sentence: "If Azureti were with us today, I would tell her. . . ." Discuss their answers.

Recall the "Four Keys" (historical perception, aftermath, social memory, and talk about God). How might these keys be used to phrase questions concerning women and miracles?

Luke: Change in the Air
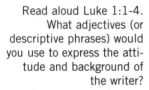

Read aloud Luke 1:1-4. What adjectives (or descriptive phrases) would you use to express the attitude and background of the writer?

Notice the writer of Luke does not profess to be an eyewitness to any of the events. Instead, he uses earlier documents and interviews. What questions might such a statement raise concerning biblical "truth" and interpretation?

Luke Gives Voice to Women
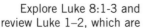

Explore Luke 8:1-3 and review Luke 1–2, which are

Luke: Change Is in the Air

Composed at the end of the first century, Luke's account of the birth, life, death, and resurrection of Jesus reads much like an eloquent novel. For instance, read Luke 1:1-4. Notice the fancy language and sentence construction. All four verses, for instance, comprise a single sentence! The writer tells the reader, Theophilus, that eyewitness accounts and other documents have been used in fashioning this account of Jesus, for the purpose of revealing "the truth concerning the things about which you have been instructed" (1:4).

"Who Was Theophilus?"

The name Theophilus *translates as "Lover of God." While a fairly popular name in the Greco-Roman world of the late first century, it does suggest that Luke writes his Gospel to a non-Jewish audience (since "Theophilus" would not be considered a Jewish name by any stretch of the imagination). But who exactly was this "God Lover"? Some scholars suggest Theophilus served as the financial benefactor who paid Luke to write his biography.*

Others assume Luke uses the name as a general way of addressing his readers: all the members of a Gentile Jesus Movement outside Palestine. Yet other persons believe "most excellent Theophilus" to have been an administrator of a Roman province. Also notice that "Acts of the Apostles," the second volume of Luke's work, addresses Theophilus by name (Acts 1:1-2).

Luke Gives Voice to Women

While the stories that follow parallel many of those narratives found in Mark and

devoted to women. Why, do you think, does Luke include these stories?

Now spend a few minutes reflecting on your life. How often to you remember to name the women whose faithful testimony gave shape to your Christian faith? If you brought photos or other mementos, talk briefly about them and their significance to you.

Name those women now through prayer, either silent or as a large group.

Jesus traveled with women he did not control. To what degree does the concept of "men owning women" find itself depicted in popular movies? the media? local churches? your personal theology?

Spend a few minutes considering other contemporary women's issues. Should men feel shame if they do not earn as much money as their wives? Why or why not? Why might they to begin with? To what extent should gender be a consideration in employment, military service, and ordination?

In what ways might suffering join persons together? Have you ever found yourself linked to another person through hardship and

Matthew, Luke's Gospel differs in a significant way: women play a predominant role throughout the entire text. The Gospel of Luke introduces us to Elizabeth, mother of John the Baptist. Luke grants a voice to Mary, mother of Jesus, as well as to Anna of the Temple (2:36-38). Luke notes that Jesus mentions at the very beginning of his ministry that Elijah, the great prophet of ancient Israel, was sent by God only to a woman, who was a widow (4:26; also see 1 Kings 17:8-24). Like Elijah's, Jesus' ministry focused upon women: their suffering, their plight, their liberation, and their salvation.

Like the prophet Elijah, Jesus came to challenge the social injustices suffered by women. Luke 8:1-3 tells us that women became permanent followers of Jesus and provided financial leadership. While modern readers might miss the radical nature of such a statement, the ancient communities would have found such a statement scandalous. Jesus traveled in the light of day with women he did not own (remember: women in the ancient world were often considered property). Further, Jesus treated these women with the same respect afforded men. Finally, he allowed himself to be financially aided by these women, who must have been wealthy (a shameful act for a man in the ancient world).

But not for Jesus. Like Elijah with the widow of Zarephath, Jesus came to *change* the rules. Through the support and guidance of women, Jesus performed many miracles, forgave the multitudes, and moved ever closer to the cross to die.

Perhaps it was the idea of suffering that brought Jesus and women together; both would understand the need to suffer, even to death, for the sake of justice. But changing the role and status of women in the ancient

oppression? Spend a few moments describing that experience. Did you sense that Jesus was a partner in that hardship? Explain.

Healing the Women

Compare Luke 8:43-48 with Mark 5:25-34. Most modern scholars assume that Luke probably had a copy of Mark. What changes does Luke make to the Markan account of this story?

Bible 301

The question of similarities and differences among Matthew, Mark, and Luke is often described as the "Synoptic Problem." Use a Bible dictionary or ask a pastor for some resources concerning a description of this unique historical and literary question concerning the Gospel accounts.

Key One: Radical Silence

How do you understand the idea of "call"? Look at Luke 5:1-11, for example. Must a call have some miraculous dimension to be legitimate? Explain.

Would you characterize the healing of this woman in Luke 8:43-48 as a call to her? Explain. What would it mean to be "a radical daughter of Christ"? In

world would bring incredible social disruption. By looking at three miracle stories found in Luke that involve women, we can see how miracles tore at the fabric of cultural standards and beliefs of the first century. I suspect these proclamations still possess the same disruptive ability, even after all these centuries.

Healing the Women in Luke

Read Luke 8:43-48, the healing of a woman who had been issuing blood for twelve years. When we compare this version of the miracle to Mark 5:25-34, we notice a major difference: the woman in Luke's account *never* articulates her reason beforehand for touching Jesus. Contrary to Mark, who describes the nameless woman as saying to herself, "If I but touch his clothes, I will be made well" (Mark 5:28), the woman in Luke remains silent. Granted, she says something to Jesus and the multitudes *after* the healing occurs (Luke 8:47), but not *before*. The reader is left wondering *why* the woman touched Jesus. Did she actually seek healing? Was she curious about the man? Did she like the texture of his garment?

Key One: Radical Silence

Using Key One (historical perception), we can find support for the reason Luke keeps the woman's reasoning private. By shifting the focus from the motivations of the woman to the actions of Jesus, this miracle functions much like a *call narrative* of Moses, of one of the prophets, or of the disciples (see in particular Luke 5:1-11, where Peter's call also occurs in the context of a miracle).

For Luke, the miracle of the woman rests within her call to become a radical

Key Two: Aftermath

your denomination, can women experience a call to ministry? Should all areas of ministry, including ordination, be open to all persons, regardless of gender, race, ethnicity, or sexuality?

Key Two: Aftermath ■

Read Leviticus 15:25-31. What do these purity laws tell you about how the woman in Luke 8 would have been regarded in her society? what her options would have been for inclusion in anything in the community?

Bible 301 □

Spend time exploring the Levitical codes surrounding sexuality and gender (Chapters 15, 18, and 20, for example). How should the modern Christian understand these codes? Should all be enforced equally? What might such codes tell us about the attitudes of the ancient world? about our own attitudes toward gender and sexuality?

Refer to the information in "Caste and Gender." To what extent should the church promote gender equality within its own practices? within society? What concrete problems might the church face in embracing such an agenda?

If a miracle affirms or reinforces gender bias in a culture, should it still be con-

daughter of Christ (Luke 8:48). Unlike the other Gospel writers, Luke fashions this miracle to declare the possibility for women in the life of the early church. Women can receive the call to ministry and become, like Peter, pillars of the faith.

Key Two: Aftermath

These miracles with women disrupt the social order. While Paul's work with the Gentiles expressed a similar notion of radical equality for women in the church (see Galatians 3:27-28), Luke's use of women in the context of miracles challenged the social status of women of the ancient world.

Read Luke 8:43-48 again. This woman must have been a member of the "untouchable" caste, the lowest social order. Banished from society, she lived as a pariah or an outcast. Read Leviticus 15:25-31. Under Jewish purity laws, this woman remained unclean (meaning unpresentable to God) indefinitely. Further, all persons whom she touched would become unclean. By entering the pressing crowd, the woman violated social and religious order. The multitudes, through this unwitting contact, had become unclean. Jesus had become unclean. For such an offense, the outcast woman could suffer death (Leviticus 15:31). Instead, she receives healing and the name of "Daughter," suggesting her inclusion into the family of Jesus. Instead of isolation, scorn, and death, the woman received new life.

Caste and Gender

Caste *refers to the clear divisions of class that exist within a society. In the ancient world, most caste systems were closed—if you were born into*

sidered a miracle? For instance, if a woman abused by a husband to the point of death inexplicably survives, only to return to the destructive relationship, has a miracle occurred? If the husband recants of his earlier hatred and bias and becomes an advocate for women, has a miracle occurred? Explain.

What are the consequences stated or implied for the healing of the woman in Luke 8? What does it mean in this story that the woman was not asked to perform any of the community ritual for purification? How does this "violation of an assumed order of the world" affect her life? the lives of others in her community? What are the implications for you?

Have you seen evidence of God "healing the system" rather than working in it? of God working in the system? Give some examples. What impact has this work of God had on you? on the system?

poverty, you stayed impoverished all of your life. Many of Jesus' actions seem to challenge the validity of such closed caste systems.

Likewise, gender roles were rigidly defined in the ancient world, but for a different reason. Women were viewed as "undeveloped" men rather than as a different gender. Due to their underdevelopment in the womb, women were destined to be subservient and dominated (or so the ancient Greeks and Romans believed). Again, Jesus' inclusion of women as followers and disciples offered a radical challenge to the gender ideas of the day.

The social and religious implications of this miracle seem incredible for its time. Through the healing of this woman, Jesus destroyed the caste system and threw into question the standard gender bias. From Jesus' perspective, this woman was no different than any other disciple. Further, she had shifted from the outer circle of society to the inner circle of Jesus. And Jesus did not require her to present herself to the Temple priests and offer the appropriate "two pigeon" sacrifice for healing. Nor does Luke report Jesus—or anybody else—holding this woman accountable for violating purity law and damaging the multitude's cleanliness. In a literal sense, the woman experiences freedom from social, religious, physical, and spiritual oppression.

Of course, the liberation of the woman only serves to magnify the oppressive nature of her culture. This miracle functions like a social "magnifying glass" through which the reader can view the disruptive nature of miracles. Like most miracles, the healing of the woman in Luke 8:43-48 violates an assumed order of the world. In the place of the standard order, Luke introduces the idea that sick and whole persons can dwell together, women and men share equally in the Kingdom's gifts, and caste systems seem unnecessary in the world.

How often does the world respond to Luke's vision for the world with the words, "No, the sick are of less social importance than the well"; "Women should be considered inferior to men"; and "God places class divisions between persons to make the poor strive harder and the rich share more"? In short: "Let's just leave the cultural, class, and gender roles as they are. Let God work within our system." Maybe the radical miracle found in Luke rests with Jesus' repudiation of this poor-thinking and human-centered arrogance. God comes to heal the system, not work within it.

Women Promote Social Memory in Miracles: Key Three

Reminding us that God does not work within the social parameters constructed by humans may be a primary role of miracles. This role has also been played by numerous Christian women throughout the centuries: Hildegarde of Bingen, Joan of Arc, Julian of Norwich, Sojourner Truth, Susanna Wesley, and many modern folks who find strength in the life stories of these women to challenge the injustices of our time. Perhaps the struggle for gender equality and justice continues to promote the disruptive nature of healing of the nameless woman in Luke. From that initial disruption, justice has sprung forth, "roll[ing] down like waters, / and righteousness like an ever-flowing stream" (Amos 5:24). And we are caught in its tide.

In some deep, significant manner, Azureti's

Women Promote Social Memory ■

Name the women within your denomination's history (or the history of Christianity) whose brave voices and behaviors challenged the theological and social conventions of their day. (For help, look on the Internet, in local libraries, or in the office of your pastor.) Have these women been models for you? If so, in what way?

Bible 301 □

Do a bit of research on the women of faith listed in the first paragraph of this section. Consult an encyclopedia or dictionary of

Christianity. Why do their names appear in this list?

In small groups of two or three persons, write a letter to Azureti. What "miracle" do you hope occurs in her life? in the lives of her church members? in the life of the two countries involved? What are the themes of liberation in Luke 8:43-48?

struggle (remember our opening story) links to the historical disruption of gender and class roles expressed in Luke. Like the interconnecting pieces of a large puzzle, this mosaic of liberation from oppression offers support and guidance to a community of sisters and brothers in Christ for whom gender, class, and sexual discrimination appears incompatible with the Christian message.

Now I understand why Azureti continued to return to the Bible, even when it was often members of her faith communities (both in Swaziland and the United States) who discounted, dismissed, and downgraded her. By reading of the women in the company of Jesus, Azureti heard the words of the ancient women: "You belong with us, Sister. We are sisters in Christ." She has experienced the third key of a miracle: social memory.

A Widow's Son

A Widow's Son ■

Read Luke 7:11-17 and 1 Kings 17:17-24. How do these events parallel each other? What would Jesus gain or lose by doing something that would remind the crowd of Elijah?

What are the events in this healing in Luke that are common to others of his healing stories? How do these common themes affect our social memory?

Imagine yourself as the widow of Nain (or of Zaraphath). Your husband is dead, and you have only one son. What are your life options? your potential sources of support? Now your son has died, and you are in the midst of his

Luke well understands the power of social memory. In Luke 7:11-17, he reports on a miraculous healing of a man who had died. What evokes social memory is the circumstance, which Luke makes abundantly clear. The deceased man was the only son of a widowed mother. Obviously she benefited greatly by the restoration of her son's life.

Luke preserves elements of this healing that he includes in his other healing stories: Jesus' compassion, his attention to those who are the most marginal or the most vulnerable in their society, Jesus' total disregard for the conventions of religious purity. That this man was the son of a widow would call to mind the miraculous healing by Elijah of the only son of a widow from Zarephath (1 Kings 17:17-24), which we have mentioned before. Luke reports that Jesus "gave him to

funeral. What would be going through your head at this moment? Then imagine that someone whom you do not know stopped the service, spoke to your son, and your son sat up, alive. Now how would you feel? What might you do? How would you regard this stranger? What is the aftermath of the healing, and how is it different from the aftermath of your son's death?

his mother" (Luke 7:15), precisely the words from 1 Kings 17:23 that referred to Elijah.

Jesus had healed before by simply stating that the ill person should be well; in other instances he touched the diseased or troubled person as well. In this instance, Jesus placed his hand on the funeral bier before commanding the man to rise. This action rendered him ritually unclean, an action sure to be noticed by the great crowd. Again, Jesus circumvented the custom and "system," bringing fear and amazement from the crowd, their praise and awe of the work of "this great prophet" (like Elijah) among them, and restoring the livelihood of a nameless "disposable" woman.

A Daughter of Abraham

Read Luke 13:10-17, Exodus 31:12-17, and Leviticus 23:1-3. What are the issues at stake in this healing miracle? Who is invested in what in the confrontation of Jesus with the synagogue authorities?

How would you describe the dichotomy of attitude between the religious leaders and the entire crowd?

The leaders reasoned that the sabbath law had been broken. Do you believe that it is permissible to defy authority or bend and break rules of society for any reason? Does your answer depend on a particular reason or type of rea-

A Daughter of Abraham

In Luke 13:10-17, Jesus heals another unnamed woman. As in the miracle narrative of the woman with the flow of blood, an "unclean" woman entered a large group of "clean" persons, causing social and religious disruption. And she received healing from Jesus and began to "praise God" (13:13). But some of the males of the synagogue, along with the lead rabbi, called into question the action of Jesus, suggesting a violation of sabbath law (see Exodus 31:12-17 and Leviticus 23:1-3). In response, Jesus rebuked them, stating that if a man would untie his ox from the feeding trough and lead it to water on the sabbath, how could they complain of his actions. The leaders were looking at the sabbath according to prohibitions, even that work on the sabbath would profane it and lead to death. Jesus viewed the sacred day as a day of life and healing.

The confrontation of Jesus with the synagogue rulers put his opponents to shame and further strengthened the social disruption.

son? Is there a point beyond which some rules or social conventions must not be violated? If so, how do you determine what those boundaries are?

How does the social and religious disruption of this and the other women's stories influence your faith? your understanding of how God works in the world? What instances, if any, of dramatic social and religious disruption can you recall? In what ways did that disruption work to serve a greater good? In what ways, and to whom, was it simply disruptive? What might our society be like if nothing ever disrupted the social or religious status quo? (Choose a date from the past, for example, and think about what it would be like to be fixated in that social, moral, ethical, political mentality, and way of being today.)

Look into the idea of being a "Daughter of Abraham." What did it mean for the woman who was healed? What might be an equivalent term today for Christians, and what impact would it have on you to be identified that way?

The "entire crowd was rejoicing at all the wonderful things that he was doing" (13:17). The synagogue, a center of religious life, continuity, and unity was instead a focus of the "us against them" relationship between what Jesus challenged as a hypocritical leadership (13:15) and the needs of the rank and file. It might be fair to say that this contest of wills was not started by this incident, but the woman's healing certainly focused attention on it.

What strikes me as most memorable about this miracle narrative is Jesus' restatement of the term *daughter* when referring to the healed woman. (See Luke 8:48 for the first instance.) This time, however, Jesus calls the woman "daughter of Abraham," summoning the very history the men of the synagogue had used to condemn the woman and her healing. By granting the unnamed woman the title "daughter of Abraham," Jesus added this woman—and her story of oppression and freedom—to the community of sisters and brothers who have fought—and will fight—this battle throughout time. Like a link in a strong chain, the story of this woman becomes the story of Azureti and all women who suffer at the hands of others.

"Women"

O God: Women today have something to say from the centuries of waiting silently. Women have found their voice in spite of the degradation suffered at the hands of an angry world. The women say: "God, why do you allow such suffering to continue? Why must women continue to taste the tears of pain rather than the fruits of compassion? How can the realm of God come to its fullness when violence, hatred, and contempt of women appear commonplace? when one rape occurs every eight seconds? when a woman dies of abuse every seventeen minutes, usually at the hands of a family member? when millions of women and children around the world starve to death each year. How long, O Lord?"

Questions for God: Key Four

Think about the implications of the three healing stories involving women. What do they prompt you to think about God and how God works in the world? in your world and life?

Read Luke 24:1-12. What does it mean to you that the women figure so prominently in the Easter morning drama? Why might women have been the first to witness the resurrection of Jesus? Why, in its own social and religious context, is this noteworthy?

Do you think that the women stood to "be the first to inherit the gifts of the Resurrection"? Explain. What does this mean?

How does the Resurrection offer hope to the world concerning life in the face of adversity and suffering? In what ways have the three women in this session's miracles "found a new home in Jesus"? In what ways has Azureti? In what ways have you?

Questions for God: Key Four

Read Luke 24:1-12, the miracle of the resurrection of Jesus. Listen to the words of the two men whom the women found in the tomb who recalled "that the Son of Man must be handed over to sinners, and be crucified, and on the third day rise again" (24:7). Of the Synoptic Gospel writers, only Luke even suggests that there might have been men present for the Crucifixion, the nameless "acquaintances" of Luke 23:49. (Matthew and Mark do not even give men this nod.) Notice how Luke (and Matthew and Mark) point out specifically the presence of the women both at the Crucifixion and on Easter morning: Mary Magdalene, Joanna, Mary the mother of James, and "the other women with them" (24:10)—a virtual communion of women. They stand as the first witnesses to the truth of Christ's resurrection.

These women also stand to be the first to inherit the gifts of the Resurrection: deliverance from the hands of their oppressors and new life in Christ. Paul's words come to mind at this point: "For if we have been united with him in a death like his, we shall certainly be united with him in a resurrection like his" (Romans 6:5).

God has heard the cries of the women of Judah. Many of the same words and actions

If you did not already do it, pray together the prayer in "Women" on pages 86-87. What theological questions does the prayer raise? How would you address them?

Read the last two sentences of this session aloud. What questions, comments, fears, and trepidations does the statement raise?

Bible 301 ☐

Review the Crucifixion and Resurrection accounts in Matthew, Mark, and Luke to compare how women are featured or mentioned by the different Gospel writers.

Closing Prayer ■

Jesus clearly included everyone, including society's lowliest citizens, in his embracing love and concern. Take time now in prayer to consider how you have responded to that welcome and either make or renew your own commitment.

Then close with your circle prayer, including prayers for justice for Azureti and others who suffer at the hands of others and for each of us to seize responsibility for being agents of God's justice, healing, and health. If you composed a prayer during the session, offer it now.

used to hurt and destroy women in Jerusalem found a new home in Jesus. In suffering, Jesus and women found common ground. In response, Luke demonstrates the new "common ground" women share with Jesus: a new life, free of oppression, hatred, and anger. While this community starts as the early Christian church, the intention seems clear—this church served as a model for the kingdom of God.

God has also heard the cries of Azureti and the countless women who suffer at the hands of others. But how will they find that "common ground" with Jesus? Surely they know the suffering. How can these women share in the joy of the Resurrection?

If the Resurrection holds meaning for modern Christians, it must be reflected in their persistence in creating the kingdom of God on earth. Failure to assist in the construction of the Kingdom surely must affect the nature of salvation. For what good is the salvation of one person if millions are lost in the process? Have we become so selfish as humans that even the gift of our salvation cannot be shared?

To the extent Christians build the Kingdom on earth, communion with the women at Christ's tomb exists. Until every woman experiences the freedom from fear of oppression, hatred, and abuse, the miracle of the Resurrection remains incomplete.

Beyond Resurrection

Session Focus ■

Miracles continue to occur in the name of Jesus. But how can Christians discern actual miracles from other "unexplained phenomena"? God manifests miracles in the world as a general declaration of power and presence rather than as a verdict on individual piety and worth.

Session Objective ■

By using the "Four Keys" to explore several of the miracle stories in Acts, participants will gain insight into how modern Christians may critique and understand God's miracles that occur in our daily lives.

Session Preparation ■

Read all of the suggested miracle narratives that are listed on pages 91-92. Using magazines, newspapers, the Internet, and other sources, find modern-day equivalents to some of these stories. As in previous sessions, make a list of the "Four Keys" visually available to participants.

Invite a local pastor or member of a congregation to speak to the participants

Recently I attended a healing service at which several persons experienced the Holy Spirit working in their midst. While encountering no dramatic cures, most persons professed a sense of "something" dwelling within them: a warming of the soul that left them feeling blissful, peaceful, and alive in Christ. Afterward, I asked many of the participants to explain what had occurred during the service. Without exception, they spoke of perceiving the Spirit of Christ entering their bodies, assessing their pain, and leaving a "mark" upon their souls. From what I could discern, the "mark" could be described as a lingering presence of the Divine that provided a new perspective on the pain and suffering of their lives.

Meet Christopher

"I know that I have been filled by the Holy Spirit . . . [t]hat God knows my suffering and offers me love through the gift of Jesus Christ," concluded Christopher, a thirty-four-year-old accountant who attended the service. "Knowing that God loves me and will never abandon me provides the foundation necessary to face the slings and arrows of daily life." When I asked Christopher, "Did a miracle occur today?" he responded quickly, "Yes, a miracle happens each time we invite the Holy Spirit into our lives to embrace our pain, dry our tears, and move

about healing services. With the assistance of trained clergy from your denomination, open the session with a healing service. Notice what elements, items, and words are used throughout the service. What assumptions does this ritual make concerning miracles and the presence of God in the world?

You will need a Bible dictionary for a "Bible 301" activity and an atlas for another.

Choose from among these activities and discussion starters to plan your lesson.

Beyond Resurrection ▪

Brainstorm insights about miracles that were revealed in previous sessions. If necessary, transfer these insights to a large piece of poster paper or a chalkboard. Consider using this list of insights as a list of criteria for discerning the value of some of the modern miracles found in local publications or media.

Meet Christopher ▪

Reflect on Christopher's response to the question, "Did a miracle occur today?" How does his answer open possibilities for what events might be considered miraculous? Can you identify any possible pitfalls or problems with his explanation?

our eyes from the pavement toward the sky." In this final session, we will explore the miracles that occurred *after* the Resurrection, as described by the writer of The Acts of the Apostles and persons like Christopher.

Jesus' Miracles Continue

While many persons may initially reject such occurrences as true "miracles of Jesus," Christian faith proclaims that Jesus' resurrection from the grave makes it possible for Christ to continue his work in the world. As Peter reminded those persons who listened to his Pentecost sermon, " 'Repent, and be baptized every one of you in the name of Jesus Christ so that your sins may be forgiven; and you will receive the gift of the Holy Spirit.' . . . Awe came upon everyone, because many wonders and signs were being done by the apostles" (Acts 2:38, 43).

For the Christian, if Jesus did not rise from the dead, the work of the early apostles would have been impossible. So it seems most appropriate to investigate these miracle narratives, looking for similarities and differences with the signs and wonders mentioned in the Gospels. Using our Four Keys (see Session One), perhaps our analysis will assist us in determining what meaning Christ's miracles hold for us today.

Acts of the Apostles: Volume Two

Composed by the same writer as Luke, The Acts of the Apostles describes the formation of the early Christian movement among the Gentiles (non-Jews). Written at the very end of the first century, the author had to deal with a few critical issues within the Gentile Jesus Movement. First, Paul, the founder of the movement, had been dead at least thirty years. While Paul's teachings

In what ways might the miracles of the modern world be connected to the actual miracles performed by Jesus?

Spend a few moments reviewing the "Four Keys" of discerning miracles, described in Session One.

Acts ■
of the Apostles ■

Why do you think Luke composed Acts of the Apostles as the continuing story of his Gospel text?

Bible 301 ☐

Using a Bible dictionary, look up the words Apocalypse, Gentile, and Paul. *What does it mean to identify a movement as non-apocalyptic? What other agenda might the church have if not preparing persons for the end of time?*

Have your encounters of Christian education focused more on preparing for the end of time or on building the kingdom of God? What specific actions might be unique to each category? What other purposes might exist for Christian education in the modern church?

Miracles Abound ■

Form several small groups and assign a different miracle to each group. Ask each group to read the account of its assigned

seemed grounded in an idea of the end of time occurring at any moment, Luke realized that such apocalyptic ideas could not be maintained indefinitely. Somehow, Paul's message of salvation through the spirit of Christ had to be recalibrated for a new generation.

Second, Paul's ideas of a "church" focused on private-home-based organizations that promised its members immortality in preparation for the end of time. By the end of the first century, the focus of these organizations shifted. No longer primarily organizations that waited for the end of time, Christian assemblies sought a new mission to the world. In many ways, the church of Paul had outlived its short-term mission of preparing for the end of the world. What should these house churches do instead?

Third, why would God delay the end of time, especially if Paul was so certain it would occur in his lifetime? Had God abandoned the house churches of Paul? By the end of the first century, a major set of theological issues arose. By leading a devout Christian to write Acts, God attempted to respond to these questions. As we shall see, the inclusion of miracle narratives within Acts assists the writer in addressing these troubling queries.

Miracles Abound

Perhaps no other book of the New Testament records such a variety of miracles occurring within the lives of the faithful. Take a look at this sampling:

- Peter heals the lame (Acts 3:1-10)
- Peter's shadow heals (Acts 5:12-16)
- Peter raises the dead Tabitha (Acts 9:36-43)
- Peter rescued from prison (Acts 12:3-19)

miracle. Record the specific ways each miracle narrative both parallels and differs from the miraculous acts of Jesus. (Further consideration of some of these parables will come later in the session.)

How important should it be for modern-day miracles to resemble the miracles of the Gospel text? For instance, can a miracle occur through modern medicine rather than the "laying on of hands"?

• Exorcism of slave-girl (Acts 16:16-18)
• Paul's hankie heals (Acts 19:11-12)
• Paul's shipwreck (Acts 27:6-44)
• No effect from snakebite (Acts 28:1-6)

Healing through handkerchiefs? Salvation through shadows? Survival of shipwrecks? Acts reads more like a special effects screenplay than a Gospel text. In fact, many scholars assume this "over-the-top" style was intentionally added by the author to grab the attention of the ancient reader. Luke wanted to declare the dramatic and powerful force of the resurrected Christ working through the movers and shakers of the early church. While some of the miracles seem to mirror acts undertaken by Jesus (for instance, compare Acts 9:36-43 with Mark 5:35-43), most appear as unique expressions within the New Testament. The dramatic nature of the miracles suggests that the Spirit that worked miracles through Jesus becomes *more powerful at the Resurrection*. The miracle-making spirit of God that dwelt in the form of Jesus now inhabits the bodies of the apostles and believers. As a result, miracles abound in Acts.

Key One: Christal at Work ■

Try your hand at writing a creative paraphrase of the healing narrative of Acts 3:1-10, composed from the perspective of the lame man. Also try constructing a paraphrase of the same story from the perspective of John and Peter. How does a shift in perspective raise new questions about this ancient text? Now compare Acts 3:1-10 with Mark 2:1-12. If Luke used Mark's story as a model for

Key One: Miracles in Acts Declare Christ at Work

Read Acts 3:1-10. Just as Jesus healed the paralytic man in Mark (see Mark 2:1-12), Peter touched a lame man, who danced for joy. As with some of the miracles of Jesus, this healing also occurs at a Temple gate and at a time when there would be a lot of traffic. It was at "three o'clock in the afternoon," a regular time of prayer and sacrifice.

The lame man, predictably, was a beggar, since he was certainly unable to work. And the "alms" he received were clearly more than he expected or bargained for. One of

this story about Peter, how did Luke shift the perspective or direction of the tale?

What historical perspective is at work here? What difference does it make now, if any?

The man was given the ability to stand and walk, which probably meant more than all the silver or gold he could imagine, and which neither all the silver and gold could purchase. What would be the one thing thought unattainable and impossible that for you would be life-altering AND show God's grace?

A Fountain of Grace

Rather than a lawn sprinkler, what other metaphors can you think of that might describe how the cross of Jesus spreads God's grace throughout the world? What value might such imagination exercises play in exploring Christian theology?

the transformational features of miracles is just that—receiving the unexpected and unanticipated, precisely what God always has to offer.

Luke (the author of Acts) uses this miracle story to make a simple, yet powerful statement. The Spirit of God found within Jesus now rests within Peter and the other apostles (including Paul). What a glorious, historical proclamation this is. The wonderful signs of God's presence did not end at the cross. Instead, the death of Jesus disseminates God's grace to the world (see John 14:11-12). This grace is priceless. As Peter said, "I have no silver or gold, but what I have I give you; in the name of Jesus Christ of Nazareth" do the one thing you believe is impossible and unattainable and that will fill your life with relief and joy: "Stand up and walk."

A Fountain of Grace

I remember spending many summer days as a child walking and running through the cool jets of water released by the lawn sprinkler in our yard. The water at times seemed to chase me, as if we were playing a variation of the game "Tag." As I grew older, and my days of running through the spraying water shortened in number, I forgot the excitement and joy of these special moments. Perhaps this image of play, however, best describes the historical proclamation that Luke makes through his telling of the miracles of the early apostles. The cross of Jesus functioned much like the sprinkler in my childhood yard. Instead of water, the cross jettisoned God's abundant possibilities and grace to a needy world. No longer isolated to the body of Jesus, the waters of grace could extend to touch the lives of all persons.

For the modern Christian, miracles

remain possible only if we continue to believe in the abundant grace made available through the cross. Perhaps my new friend Christopher understood that concept better than I did. Through God's grace, wonderful things have occurred. Wonderful things *will* occur. And, like the water games of my childhood, the grace of God may be unpredictable, soaking us at the most unexpected times in the most unsuspecting of places. Maybe at a worship service, but maybe while you sit in your car at a drive-through window waiting for a food order. Maybe through a pastor or healer, but maybe through the actions of a stranger or physician. Like the lame man who begged Peter for money but found health instead, I find myself receiving blessings from God usually when I *least* expect it. Hopefully, when such miracles occur, I will have the forethought to leap up and praise God (Acts 3:8).

Do you have confidence that wonderful things will occur? Why or why not? What was the most unsuspecting place or occasion on which something wonderful, gracious, or miraculous happened to you? Describe that experience and what it meant to you.

Key Two: Miracles Should Disturb Our World

Read Peter's sermon, delivered immediately following the healing of the lame man (Acts 3:11-26). Peter reiterated that the healing occurred not by the "power and piety" of the apostles but by the "the faith that is through Jesus" (3:12, 16). Further, Peter proclaimed that the "times of refreshing" (see 3:20; like water from a yard sprinkler) have come to the world through Christ's suffering on the cross. While Moses, Samuel, and the prophets of the Old Testament also disseminated the refreshing waters of grace, the death of Christ makes such grace (and the wonders it can work) available to the entire world.

Well, the priests, Temple leaders, and Sadducees quickly understood the disruptive

Key Two ■

Many modern biblical scholars point out the unique theology in Peter's sermon: that the members of Peter's audience had Jesus killed through an act of misguided justice (Acts 3:14-15). To find forgiveness for this heinous act, they should follow Jesus. Read Acts 3:11-26. Notice the absence of the idea of salvation through the death of Jesus. For Luke, the Resurrection provided an opportunity for the naughty folks to get it right the second time. How does Peter's reasoning for the death and resurrection of Jesus parallel your own understanding?

Read Acts 4:1-4. Why might Peter and John wish to amass an army of five thousand men? Why, do you think, would the Temple authorities object to their teaching and to the conversion of all those people?

What are the disruptive features of the passages you have read so far? How has the aftermath of these events affected the persons involved? What difference does that make now, if any?

Peter's Great Escape ■

Read Acts 12:3-19 aloud and slowly enough so that everyone can visualize all the details and events as they unfold. Keep in your mind's eye the spectacle at the prison when the angel appeared and the confusion at Mary's house when Peter showed up in the middle of the night. Note how the most harsh and cavalier part of the story— Herod having guards executed with a word and then going off to his vacation spot in Caesarea—is given just two sentences.

potential of the healing miracle. If the people believe in this wonderful act (and Peter's interpretation of it), the Jewish community may well have a new competitor for spreading the grace of God.

Read Acts 4:1-4. The social and religious disruption of this single miracle led to the arrest of Peter and John. It also led to the formation of a band of five thousand male followers of Peter (to recall the significance of this number, review Session Five). It seems as if this single action— the unexpected healing of a lame man—has brought about social unrest and disorder.

By definition, miracles disrupt and disturb the expected order of things. Modern Christians often find themselves praying to God for a miracle, but asking that such displays of grace fit cleanly within the lines of human expectations and social structures. It is as if we say, "God, I want a miracle, but please do not disrupt my life in the process." Miracles can bring incredible disorder and chaos, leaving lives in the wake of significant transformation and ambiguity.

Peter's Great Escape

The miraculous escape of Peter from prison has all the marks of disorder, chaos, transformation, ambiguity, and even a little humor. Read Acts 12:3-19. Note the extraordinary measures used to contain one man: bound with *two* chains, attended by *two* guards within the cell and other guards outside the cell—*four* squads. Herod was determined to keep Peter in jail; God was determined to let him out.

Somehow, Peter managed to sleep with his heavy and painful chains and "roommates" right beside him. An angel appeared, shone a light on him, "tapped" him to awaken him, (other translations say, "struck"), and off

Apply the first two keys. What is the historical perspective in this story for the original audience and for you? What is the aftermath, and how did it affect the key characters? How does it matter to you?

How do you handle the chaos, ambiguity, and disruption that God's intervention can impose in your life?

dropped the chains. Evidently the guards didn't hear or see a thing, even while the doors swung open and Peter glided out past all those squads of guards.

Upon arriving under cover of darkness at the home of some believers, Peter banged at the gate to be let in. Rhoda was so flustered at seeing him that she slammed the door in his face and ran back to tell the others what she had seen. Fortunately they recovered their senses enough to let him in.

From the angel poking him awake to the prison doors blowing open to the comedy of errors at Mary's house, this miracle seems humorous. But the chaos and cavalier death of the innocent guards the next morning (12:18-19) aren't funny. This miracle definitely disturbed somebody's world.

Christopher's Release

How might you provide counsel and strength to Christopher? What theological questions might his description of recent events raise?

Again, my friend Christopher has been of great assistance to me. While his experience did not take anyone's life, it certainly included risk and loss. When asked to describe a recent miracle of the Holy Spirit, Christopher shared this story:

"Work had been a real bummer. So much stress, so many clients. And when people experience anxiety concerning their money, it only compounds the problems. I found myself becoming sick, both physically and spiritually. My roommate noticed my sour mood and disposition and suggested that I take my concerns to God in prayer. Well, nothing happened, at least not immediately. A few days later, though, during a lunch break, I felt something "break" inside me, like a water balloon full of some warm liquid. My disposition changed, my spirit shifted, and my flu-like symptoms disappeared.

"While joy flooded my heart, my boss

If miracles cause such social, spiritual, and physical disruptions, why do Christians pursue them with such vigor? Can "disturbance" and "disruption" promote any positive feelings, ideas, or dimensions? Explain.

flooded my ears . . . with criticism. She told me I had 'lost my edge' and spent too much time thinking about the lives of clients rather than the health of the firm. Last week I received my 'pink slip.' I guess gifts can have many sides."

Without exception, Christ-centered miracles bring about social, economic, political, religious, and emotional change. Things just do not stay the same. Violations of standard expectations and world-views can often bring periods of discomfort, ambiguity, and even doubt to the believer. Do such disruptive experiences undermine the value of miracles within our lives? Absolutely not. But this much-overlooked dimension of the miracle experience forces us to clarify the events in our lives—and the lives of others—that qualify as miracles.

Do you think that God would let someone be hurt through a miracle? (Remember the guards of Peter.) How do you reconcile God's grace and the disruptive impact or risk of some of God's miracles?

Further, the "aftermath" dimension establishes the "ripple effect" of miracles: the more forceful the miracle, the more far-reaching the disturbance. For instance, the world still vibrates from the death of Jesus on the cross. We find ourselves caught in its aftermath, watching the world change around us. For Christopher, the miracle of healing led to a release from employment, increased financial hardships, and perhaps some tension at home. So does God intend Christopher—or any of us—to hurt through miracles? Of course not. But change comes at the price of comfort. And change rests at the core of the Christian miracle.

Key Three: Modern Miracles Remember Christ

Key Three ■

Saints can refer to both those persons who live a life dedicated to Christ (see Ephesians 2:19-22, for instance) and those special persons

As we have already encountered, several of the miracles described within Acts resemble works of Jesus: healing the sick, raising the dead, curing the lame, and exorcising the

throughout history who practiced Christian faith to epic or historic levels. Which definition does your denomination promote? Should the saints of the Christian tradition be venerated; that is, remembered and honored as sacred models for modern lives?

Name the "saints" in your life: those persons whose Christian lives serve as a model for your own walk with God. In what way do these lives serve as a miracle to the Christian community?

possessed. The author calls upon this parallel to remind both ancient and modern readers of another fundamental principle concerning Christian miracles—such events should lead us to recall the stories of the faithful.

Read the words of Peter's sermon once again (Acts 3:11-26). The healing of the lame man leads the one called "The Rock" to rehearse the wonderful acts of God throughout history. Further, Peter seeks to demonstrate how this single incident of rejuvenation fits within the larger scheme of God's plan: to offer salvation to the entire world.

"Why Is Peter a Rock?"

While Matthew 16:18 states, "And I tell you, you are Peter, and on this rock I will build my church," many modern-day Christians fail to understand the playfulness behind the statement. In Greek, the original language of the New Testament, Petros *(the name expressed in English as "Peter") sounds like the word for "rock,"* petra. *The early audience for Matthew would have relished the love and intimacy such name-play suggested. What modern "name games" do you play to show adoration and love to somebody?*

How, after all this study of miracles, would you define what a miracle is or is not? Has your definition changed? If so, how? Is there any difference, do you think, between a mystery and a miracle? If so, what is it?

Inexplicable events happen in our world each day. People recover from cancer. A child survives a terrible automobile accident. Weather patterns change dramatically. While persons may be tempted to identify each one of these occurrences as a "miracle," only those experiences that bring to mind the work of the saints of the Old Testament, New Testament, and universal church would qualify, theologically speaking. While not to discount the value of such mysteries, Christians use the term *miracle* to say, "This wondrous event fits into the history of such events as professed by the Christian faith."

The theological and historical significance of the term *miracle* has been eroded by secular folks. Now the term means anything from "changed opinions" to "altered attitudes." Key Three suggests that Peter and Paul's approach as recorded in Acts seems most appropriate. If the mysterious event draws us back to the stories, testimonies, and proclamations of the Christian faith, then it should be considered a continuation of God's work in the world, hence, a miracle. If not, let it simply be called a mystery, a wonder, an unexplainable phenomenon.

A Shadow Without a Doubt

I read recently about a woman who discovered that a shadow cast on her refrigerator door between the hours of 6:00 P.M. and dusk resembled—at least in her perception—an image of Jesus. Within days of its discovery, hundreds of persons flocked to the home of this devout Christian, paying homage to the shadow that appeared nightly. Several persons reported being physically and spiritually transformed by the apparition. Others, less touched, found the entire endeavor silly. In fact, once somebody chopped down a pear tree that stood just outside the kitchen window, the shadow of Jesus disappeared.

Was this event a miracle? In the sense that the shadow served as a means by which to rehearse the stories of faith, yes. Recall the story of the woman healed of the flow of blood (Mark 5:25-34) who felt she would be healed simply by touching Jesus' hem. Recollect the story of the belief in the heal-

Is there any difference, do you think, between a mystery and a miracle? If so, what is it?

A Shadow Without a Doubt ▪

Read Acts 5:12-16 and 19:11-12. Recall the events of the healing of the woman with a flow of blood (Mark 5:25-34).

Form four small groups and assign one of the keys to each group. Have each group analyze the "Shadow of Jesus" story from the perspective of its key. After several minutes, come together as a larger group to share your results, questions, and insights.

If Jesus' hem, Paul's handkerchief, or Peter's shadow can bring a miraculous healing through some kind of contact, can this shadow on the refrigerator be efficacious somehow? Explain.

How do you discern the difference between authentic spiritual impact and the foolish reverence of some icon, symbol, or charm?

ing power of Paul's possessions (Acts 19:11-12). Review the report that even Peter's shadow had curative power for those who believed it would (5:12-16). While we do not engage in magical thinking that wishing will make something so, should this woman's shadow of Jesus be regarded differently?

Well, you might respond, does not the chopping down of the tree demonstrate the absurd nature of such events? Not really. Given this single key of discernment (that miracles must serve as a form of memory for God's people), the woman's refrigerator door seems to be a perfect site for a miracle. I do wonder how well this modern event, however, holds up under the scrutiny of Keys One and Two: miracles as proclamations of theological history and with an aftermath of social disruption. What exactly did the event proclaim about God's presence in the world? How did this event bring about social disruption for the sake of the kingdom of God? Perhaps our use of the fourth key—miracles raise questions concerning God—could serve as another level of critique. True Christian miracle or just an odd set of occurrences? You be the judge.

Key Four ■

Read Acts 28:1-10. What were the ways that Paul's snakebite was interpreted?

In this case, the reasoning was either one of retributive justice (bad things happen to bad people, and so on) or of religious mystery (he must be a god). Today, we would probably consider the second stance as magical thinking. What about the first? How do you

Key Four: Miracles Raise Divine Questions

Read Acts 28:1-10. Shipwrecked on the island of Malta, Roman prisoners, guards, and Paul found this paradise full of friendly persons but hidden dangers. In particular, a poisonous snake bit Paul on the hand while he gathered firewood (28:3). The citizens, observing this event, offered two possible reasons why such a tragedy had occurred to this island newcomer. First, they contended that the gods intended Paul to die in the shipwreck for his evil deeds. Somehow, Paul

reason through the question of why bad things happen? Do you ask any "why" questions at all when good things happen? Explain.

Bible 301 ☐

Use an atlas to locate Malta. How might you find information concerning the history of this ancient island culture? During the time of Paul, Malta served as a Roman-occupied trading post, producing textiles and honey. The wonderful seascapes, culture, history, and climate make this collection of islands a popular vacation spot for Europeans.

If miracles serve as general, public announcements of God's work in the world, why do so many Christians interpret these events as private verdicts on the value and worth of individuals?

How would you respond to the comment, "If miracles exist as examples of divine justice, then most persons on the planet must be damned"?

What does this miracle, the aftermath of its witnesses, and your current interpretation of that event tell you about the persons involved? about God?

escaped judgment. With the help of the snake, Paul would meet his destiny. When Paul shook the snake off his hand and failed to become sick or die, a second reason came to mind: Paul must be a god (28:6). This idea appeared confirmed by Paul's later behavior, for he spent the next three months healing the diseased citizens of Malta (28:7-10).

I have heard the reasoning of the citizens of Malta evoked within my own community on numerous occasions. Good things must happen to good persons; bad things must happen to bad persons. Bitten by a snake? Well, you must have deserved it. Managed to live? Well, God must yet need you for something. Such logic seems to tell me more about the beliefs of the speaker than the nature of God, however.

My work with miracles, both ancient and modern, offers two insights. First, miracles should raise new avenues of discovery concerning the nature of God and God's intentions for the world. If miracles serve as *general announcements* from God concerning God's unfolding plan (rather than specific pronouncements of the worth or value of any given individual), then such events should say something unique, different, perhaps alarming. If miracles exist as examples of divine justice, most persons on the planet must be damned. Fortunately, the gospel of Jesus Christ and the works of the saints do not promote such a notion. In fact, as our work in previous sessions demonstrates, Jesus' miracles liberate and transform.

Think of the startling question to the citizens of Malta. Was Paul really a god? Such a theological inquiry shook the foundations of their polytheistic faith. Imagine their response when Paul explained that, while he was not a god, he performed miracles through the spirit of the God who had dwelt with the people of the earth for generations. The miracles of health and wholeness led to discovering a new dimension of faith, not possible through any other means.

Miracles in Full Relief

Miracles in Full Relief ■

Read Acts 17:22-31. Perhaps the "miracle" rests in Paul's sermon; the naming of the "unknown god" provides the radical breaking of the status quo. Sometimes miracles come in the form of enlightenment, available only to those persons who listen.

Think about the miracles discussed in this session or any of the others included in this study book. How have the four keys illuminated the miracle stories for you? What insights have you gained about how God worked (and continues to work) through miraculous events? How do you think theologically about what it means when a miracle happens to one, but not to another?

Read Acts 17:22-31, Paul's sermon to the crowds in Athens. Notice: miracles do *not* occur in Athens. Consequently, people do not believe in Paul's testimony (with the rare exceptions of Dionysius, a woman named Damaris, and a few nameless others). Miracles of God must not only shatter the status quo; they must raise new questions concerning the power, nature, and intent of the Living God.

The Book of Acts demonstrates the four keys of Christian miracles in full relief. Historically, miracles of the Christ must make historical proclamations concerning faith; their aftermath disrupts the social and religious order; they function as the memory of the Christian family; and they raise new, provocative questions concerning the nature of God. I wonder to what extent the modern Christian uses such keys to discern the mysterious events of the day? How do we separate the unexplainable phenomena of science and technology from the exploding presence of God in the world? Are we still trapped with a Malta-like system of believing miracles speak to individual piety, or have we moved to proclaiming miracles as God's general revelation to the world of critical identity and purpose?

Any Day for Miracles

Any Day for Miracles ■

Read Christopher's critique of this session. How do his ideas and feelings compare with your own insights and questions?

I asked Christopher to read my thoughts on modern miracles. I thought you might enjoy reading his response:

How do you distinguish "the everyday variety of unexplained stuff from the intentional acts of God"?

"I never thought about miracles this way. Sure, Christians should have a way to distinguish the everyday variety of unexplained stuff from the intentional acts of God. And I never thought about it before, but perhaps my focus on miracles has always been a bit self-serving and self-centered. Perhaps true miracles are gifts to the whole family of God and just not the individual. I used to think of miracles as verdicts on my piety. Instead, this session has introduced me to a radically different understanding. A lot to think about."

So, I leave you with your thoughts. I believe God works miracles within our world every day. Given the appropriate tools of discernment, we can identify those divine actions and hear the voice of God calling us toward the Kingdom.

Closing Prayer

Jesus Christ is clearly still at work in the world and we have an open invitation to both participate in and be blessed by that work. Take time now in prayer to consider your relationship to Jesus Christ and then either make or renew your covenant.

Close with your circle prayer, followed by this unison prayer: "God, sometimes we wander in the deserts of life, looking for a sign of your presence. Help us experience you through the works and wonders of others. We pray for a miracle, God, each time we lift our eyes to the sky and look for you. Move our hearts to find the Christ within each person we encounter; then, perhaps, we will find the miracle for which we seek. Amen."